Beyond Good Manners
How to Raise a Sophisticated Child

Tara Woods Turner, CEP
J. Blake Turner, PhD

This book is dedicated to the beloved memory of Deborah Woods Chambers, whose grace and beauty have inspired us from day one.

Acknowledgements

We wish to thank our beautiful, endlessly fascinating nieces and nephews - Eric, Jessie, Kayla, Mimi, Caleb, Liam and Tara Naomi - our adoration resonates through every page of this book.

To Charlie and Sam - You live your lives with meaning and truth and it is an honor and a joy to see the men you've become.

To our amazing godchildren - Ty, A'Lexus, Kenyon, Shay, Theo Jr., Triveace, Rebecca, Lebron, Quentin, Alexandra, Joshua and Iyesha - our lives are so much sweeter because of you and we thank you.

Many of us learn most of our parenting from those who raised us. Thus, we owe a huge debt of gratitude to Deborah, Grace and Jay, who cared about who we would be in the world.

Table of Contents

Introduction

You are relaxing at a neighborhood cafe on a Saturday afternoon. Sipping your beverage, you observe two separate families having lunch. In the first family a boy is dunking chicken nuggets into a ramekin of ketchup as he laughs hysterically at something he sees on his cell phone. He's wearing jeans, an oversized hockey jersey and the latest basketball sneakers. As they prepare to leave, he bounds for the door as his mom clears away their trash and his dad gets in line at the register to pay.

In the second family a boy is enjoying a grilled chicken salad, his free hand and his napkin resting in his lap. He is asking his mom if her visits to the new chiropractor have been going well. He is wearing jeans, a casual polo shirt and a pair of leather deck shoes. After their meal he hands his mom her sweater from the back of her chair and helps his dad clear the table.

We have no way of knowing if the first boy is generally rude, unkempt or thoughtless. He may very well be an obedient child, a good student and a kind and caring friend. Yet the second child clearly possesses something else besides these admirable qualities that make a distinct impression.

You are a teacher helping a group of children working on Mother's Day cards in a fourth grade art class. Most of the kids are pasting roses and hearts onto folded squares of construction paper. You notice one child is carefully tearing her paper into small squares and sorting them by color. When you ask her what she is arranging she excitedly tells you that she is constructing a mosaic of her mother's favorite flowers - lilies - and with any luck it will look a little bit like a Monet when it is completed.

The hearts and roses kids are probably sweet, wonderful children who definitely want to please their mothers with thoughtful cards. It is just as clear, however, that the little girl attempting the

1

Monet reproduction is bringing something different and unique to the enterprise.

Two teenagers are shopping for prom dresses on a Saturday afternoon. While navigating the busy streets downtown the first girl spots a group of people examining knock-off designer handbags being sold by a sidewalk vendor. Thrilled, she urges the second teen to help her pick out a purchase. The second teen says that she doesn't think it is a good idea, explaining the infringement and labor issues involved with black market production and where the profit from such activity likely ends up. She then links arms with her friend and tells her she knows of a really great shop within walking distance that sells well-made leather goods at decent prices.

The sophisticated child is mature, but she is much more than that. The loud chicken nugget kid in our restaurant scene might well be mature. After all, many adults these days consistently dress down and speak on cell phones in public settings, and most of them are reliable individuals who hold down jobs and shoulder their responsibilities with integrity. In addition to any apparent maturity, however, the other boy in the restaurant is also considerate, well-groomed and is observing a level of etiquette that is surely making his family's dining experience more enjoyable.

Do children naturally behave like the sophisticated young man in the cafe? It is far more likely that his kind and courteous behavior was conscientiously taught to him by his parents. For example, while almost all kids want their parents to be free from pain, this young man has learned to temporarily remove himself from his own personal concerns to consider his mother's well-being. Similarly, most children would, like the second boy in the story, choose the hockey jersey or something else commonly worn by peers because "that's what kids do". With input from parents, however, a child will learn to care about his appearance and chose clothing that is tidy, attractive and appropriate. The tools necessary to develop these characteristics in your own child are thoroughly inventoried in this book.

To the vignette involving the Mother's Day cards one might say "let kids be kids - why should they know about Monet? " To this we answer, "why shouldn't they?" If your child enjoys pretty pictures, then a Monet print is simply another type of pretty picture. This awareness makes the little girl's art project not only fun but an extension of her education in art.

Was our socially conscious teen in the third scenario an incredible killjoy to interfere with her friend's plans to buy the knock-off handbag? Certainly not. It is true that if one is not considerate, sharing knowledge about sweatshop working conditions can be seen as preachy or snobby. But as we will discuss in later chapters, the sophisticated youth knows how to make others feel at ease in conversation regardless of the points being made.

Today's parents want their children to possess more than good grades, more than athletic ability and more than basic common courtesies. They envision children who are comfortable with responsibility, take ownership of their experiences and rise to the occasion with maturity and style. These goals are not only admirable but attainable - we are ready to show you how.

Baby boomers, grandparents, gen x'ers and millennials want the best possible outcomes for their families. Aside from being better educated than any other generation in US history, today's parents are diverse, socially savvy, outcome-oriented consumers. Their decisions are well thought out and are based upon their aspirations. And what do parents state is their single biggest concern and the motivation behind their choices? The well-being of their children.

If you are reading this book you understand this and you are certainly not alone. Parents are constantly searching for ways to improve their child rearing approach. Of all websites frequented by moms, Pinterest, Instagram and online parenting communities consistently rank in the top five. While it's true that parents are inspired and entertained by social media they also feel the pressure to have the perfect family life and are turning to the internet to see how other parents are getting the job done.

So what, precisely, is a sophisticated child? Such a child has been exposed to more ideas than have most children and confidently seeks out more to explore. She is independent, but does not use her autonomy to overwhelm others less confident than she and she appreciates the wisdom of her parents and other adults in her life. She has not been fawned over - she has been validated. She has not been spoiled - she has had the benefit of her parents' time and resources. She has not been taught to act like an adult - she has been taught to behave well.

The sophisticated child does her best and presents her best self, at any age. She has not been shielded from reality - she has been given age appropriate tools to mature organically and make informed decisions.

The parents of sophisticated children understand that success is facilitated by experience. They look for every opportunity to give their child these experiences to help her grow. These parents know that a child cannot be competent without being confident in her abilities. They set worthy goals for their child because they realize that she becomes stronger by the efforts to achieve them, regardless of success or failure.

Not all sophisticated children are alike. Some may take an early interest in Shakespeare if they are exposed to him, while others will prefer comic books. (In the case of the latter we say at least buy them really good comic books) Some may be adept at playing an instrument while others find lessons a chore. Beyond certain premises that are covered in detail in this book, the precise details of what your child learns and is interested in are not our focus. What is important is that your child has been taught to learn, that you have made the process accessible and enjoyable and she has the confidence to engage new ideas and experiences throughout her life.

We will consistently challenge you to raise your expectations of both yourself and of your child regardless of her current age. It is beneficial to begin exploring concepts and then activities with your child that may seem a year or so beyond her developmental stage. It is only "too soon" for a new idea or skill if one is overly invested in the immediate outcome. Exposure creates the framework for eventual comprehension and involvement. Throughout this book, we will encourage you to involve your child in tasks that she certainly will not be ready to master.

You will be both proud and pleased as you discover she can absorb much more than you originally thought possible.

The sophisticated child inevitably earns the respect and admiration of peers, educators and others in her community. Eventually she will take the lead in her personal development and a lifelong desire to grow and explore will be the satisfying result. We know this to be true: the benefits for your child will far exceed the effort you will expend to realize them and the memories you make along the way will be priceless.

Each chapter in this book deals with a particular area of behavior or social interaction that is important for the development of the sophisticated child. Each chapter discusses the skills and knowledge necessary to display sophistication in that particular area. Each chapter also provides concrete suggestions for ways to impart these skills in a manner that is fun for both you and your child.

Gendered pronouns are alternated among the chapters. (He/him- she/her). This is done to keep the information flowing smoothly and is not intended to assign gender specificity to any of the topics being covered. Equally, the word 'parent' is used exclusively but with the respectful understanding that this can refer to and include legal guardians, grandparents, foster parents, nannies and other individuals who may be important or continual caregivers.

As you follow the information and advice in this book, it is important to remember that the sophisticated child you want will not materialize overnight. Your teen may not replace all of her jeans with pencil skirts or take up yachting. You can rest assured, however, that your child will respond to the instruction you provide, especially if you are consistent and model the behaviors we discuss yourself.

There is a quality sophisticated people have in common. It is something like elegance, an air of stature and accomplishment that inspires admiration and a desire to emulate it. We happily assume you are reading this book because you have observed this certain something in others -- perhaps you possess it yourself -- and you definitely want it for your child. We shamelessly do not mind telling you, good parent, that you have come to the right place. Beyond Good Manners: How to Raise a Sophisticated Child is the resource to which parents can refer time and again as their children mature. The approach and suggestions presented here will be effective when your child is five years old and when he is borrowing the family car at 16.

Let's get started, shall we?

Chapter 1
Etiquette: An Overview

"Nothing is less important than what fork you use. Etiquette is the science of living. It embraces everything. It is ethics. It is honor."
Emily Post

The sophistication you work to instill in your child will be most evident in her excellent manners and sense of decorum. They will add grace and style to every aspect of her life, letting others know that she respects herself and those around her.

Etiquette is a system whose sole purpose is to allow us to be comfortable and competent in our social role. A bit of history may provide insight. Although the word etiquette is French in derivation the history of etiquette as a practice goes back millennia. Tablets have been discovered in Egypt with recorded instructions on proper behavior and manners. In some of his writings the philosopher Confucius included suggestions on the best way to dine in the company of others. Many cultures around the world established rules about best practices and models of behavior, but we give credit to the French for the universal codification of said rules into a uniform, widely acknowledged canon of social do's and don't's. The word etiquette initially meant property or, more literally, a label affixed to property to indicated contents and ownership (from the middle French infinitive estiquer meaning "to put" or "to place"). Usage of the term as pertaining to manners began in the 18th century as authors worked to put the social habits of the aristocracy in writing. The newly enriched upper middle class were anxious to learn and imitate the behavior and practices of the aristocracy. Books on the rules of etiquette were advanced as valued guides to acceptable behavior and comportment. The rules themselves, of course, predate these books. In earlier eras, behavioral customs allowed for a uniform approach to social interactions, eliminating ambiguity and uncertainty. The odds of giving or receiving offense grew comfortably slimmer. This was especially important in times when even a minor insult to the wrong person could have dire consequences.

For example, the dinner knife was invented by an English aristocrat who surmised that a blunted knife devoted solely to dining would cut down (no pun intended) on dangerous misunderstandings between dinner guests. At that time in history few men traveled without a dagger and it was common to use it to cut one's meat at meals. Pointing a dagger at another, however, was taken as an insult and a challenge and the results were often catastrophic. The invention of the dinner knife changed the way people interacted with one another at table - etiquette followed form which followed function.

Having rules of conduct that were organized and known to all also allowed people to be more at ease in their social interactions -- there was no guesswork as to acceptable behavior. For example, the rules for cross-gender introductions stipulated that males should be introduced to females. Thus, a lady who received the introduction of a gentleman could be sure she would not have to work up the nerve to make a new acquaintance or be seen as pushy or over-eager. In addition, she was relieved from the burden of determining which men her family considered to be appropriate conversation partners.

One of the most persistent misconceptions about etiquette is that it is meant to distinguish people with status from others in order to assert a sense of superiority. This attitude, however, actually shows a regrettable lack of etiquette and is a sure sign that such a person does not truly understand good manners. There is nothing sophisticated about making others feel awkward or ill at ease. By putting the principles of this chapter into practice you will be pleased to see your child develop in a way that lets her best, most considerate self shine through.

In your efforts to raise a child who is courteous and considerate, setting a good example will be key. Most often, however, additional effort on your part will be necessary. For younger children role playing is an excellent way to teach manners. Make younger children honorary instructors and give them the task of teaching good manners to their dolls, puppets or action figures. Eventually let them take the lead as they grow increasingly comfortable with these lessons.

Older children may need the occasional gentle reminder with respect to their manners, but it is also important to provide social opportunities that allow them to practice. Give them encouragement as they learn. It is natural to correct something a child is doing incorrectly but praise is also a positive reinforcement when a child executes a task accurately. There are a multitude of excellent books, DVDs, classes and summer workshops that will show you how to teach good manners to your child in more detail than we cover here. Pick the ones that have proven results and are a good fit for your child's age and preferred learning style. Before long you will have a positively posh and perfectly polite child!

Chapter 2
Making Introductions and Taking Leave

"Give warm greetings and farewells. I was surprised at how much this resolution changed the atmosphere of my home."
Gretchen Rubin

It is always a good idea to introduce your child to new acquaintances. It gives him a chance to practice his manners and can help to alleviate the natural shyness and anxiety children often feel around new people. Young children experience varying degrees of stranger stress and, as it affords them a measure of protection, you do not want to discourage this tendency altogether. It is best then to assure your child that you think it would be wonderful if he made the acquaintance of Mr. or Ms. Dinner Guest, sending him the signal that you condone the meeting and that he can let his guard down.

Your child should offer his right hand to the person to whom he is being introduced. It will be difficult for him at first, but encourage him to maintain eye contact during the introduction. When your child is older, looking down or at anything other than the person with whom he is speaking will give the impression that he is distracted, insecure or guarded. These qualities do not inspire regard or trust in others. If you happen to introduce your child to more than two people at a time he should refrain from shaking hands altogether. A polite nod in the group's direction will do just fine. It is not necessary for him to introduce himself as you will have already done so along with informing both parties of the others' names and relationship to you.

Children should always refer to any adults by their honorific or title and their surname. The only exceptions are when the child has been given permission to use another name or if the name is not known to the child. In the latter instance a simple address of sir or ma'am is sufficient. The goal is not to prevent him from having a sense of acquaintanceship with adults. Rather, this degree of formality teaches him that it is the adult who sets the tone and example of social interaction. He cannot absorb this message if he develops the habit of calling adults by whatever name he decides is best. It displays a lack of courtesy that will not do your child any favors as he matures.

Once your child has been introduced, it is only necessary then for him to say "How do you do?" If asked the same, he should respond with "Fine, thank you. I hope you are, as well." or something similar.

It is perfectly natural for the adults in the conversation to ask the child questions that he can answer easily and comfortably. For young children, it is okay to prompt them by reminding them of whatever little details are necessary to answer someone's question. This tells them that they can depend on you in a pinch and that their security is important. We do not want our children to perform for company, but rather, to become accustomed to being around adults. When children are exposed to conversation at a young age they will soon become at ease with it and add to the conversation without prompting.

Do not expect or require your child to make small talk if it is out of character for him to do so. It will not make him skilled at small talk, but will only make him anxious at the very mention of an impending get-together. Shy children often outgrow their bashfulness and they should be allowed the space to do so.

If your child is naturally confident and outgoing it is important that you strike a balance between encouraging his friendliness and teaching him not to overwhelm others with his vivacity. If he should forget himself and monopolize the attention of an adult for too long, simply join the conversation and cheerfully but gradually wind the discussion down until you can engage him in another activity. You will have just succeeded in giving him a valuable cue about polite communication and he will absorb it in time. In the meantime continue to reinforce the point that listening is as important as speaking.

If you are giving a party or hosting a gathering let your child assist you. He can show guests where they can put their coats or the location of the powder room. If your guest is familiar to your child encourage him to extend a warm greeting with either a handshake or, when appropriate, a hug accompanied by an indication that he is glad to see the individual again.

When taking leave your child should again offer his hand and if the individual is a new acquaintance express that it was nice to meet him. It is okay to prompt young children in this nicety with a quick whisper. Honesty is always the best policy so if your child had a particular reason why he did not enjoy the company of a guest, he should simply shake hands and thank him for coming, simply omitting any indication that he enjoyed the meeting or hopes to meet again soon.

An intention to hug anyone, even family members, should be preceded by a request to do so. This teaches your child that personal spaces are to be respected and that physical contact is not always welcomed by some people, despite the good intentions of the giver. With experience this habit will become second nature and for every ten people who find the request unnecessary there will be one who is grateful for being extended the courtesy of having a say in the matter.

Your child should be expected to introduce friends and acquaintances to you if you have yet to meet them. If you begin to teach these courtesies to him at an early age he will become expert at making the principals in an introduction at ease. This affords him all of the sophistication that mastery of these skills provides.

There are several things to keep in mind when making an introduction:

Males are always introduced to females and younger people are always introduced to older people. When there is a conflict between these two considerations, gender takes precedence over age. A child would introduce his friend Liam to grandfather, but he would introduce grandfather to his friend Naomi.

If your child introduces one person to two or more people the group should be introduced to the individual. Your child would first ask his friend Debbi if he may introduce her to his classmates. This should be done as discreetly as possible, preferably out of the hearing of the group. If Debbi was preparing to leave or has a headache, for example, she will feel obliged to go through with the introduction if you ask her in front of others. If she agrees to the introduction your child would then tell his classmates that he would like them to meet his friend, Debbi. He would then tell Debbi he would like for her to meet his classmates Sam, Charlie, Jessica and Eric.

When arriving at anyone's home for a social engagement the first thing to do is locate and greet the host and guest of honor, in that order. If his grandparents are hosting an anniversary party for his aunt and uncle your child should greet his grandparents first, his aunt and uncle next and then mingle with the other guests. When attending a function an older child can give the host or hosts a small token of his regard such as an inexpensive spray of flowers or a scented candle.

One should not leave any gathering or party without locating both the host or hostess and guest of honor. Teach your child that if he has enjoyed the event he should express that to them along with a handshake. If that is not the case and he did not have a good time he should simply thank them warmly for inviting him and shake hands. You child may not have had fun, but his hosts will only remember his decorum and impeccable manners.

Chapter 3
Courtesy and Comportment

"Courage. Kindness. Friendship. Character. These are the qualities that define us as human beings, and propel us, on occasion, to greatness."
R.J. Palacio

Etiquette is demonstrated by the concern for the comfort of others in a social setting. A few simple guidelines can help your child become someone whose company is sought after and genuinely enjoyed.
Common Courtesy Basics
Although not by any means exhaustive, this list can serve as the foundation upon which your child will build a tactful communication style over the years.

Please: When requesting an item or action from another.

Thank you: After receiving an item from another, when someone has complied with a request, or after learning of someone's consideration of you.

Bless you: After a sneeze or following an especially kind word or deed from others.

Pardon or excuse me: When it is necessary to interrupt or contradict someone and, of course, after you sneeze or cough. Also should be said while crossing in front of someone, before passing near someone who may be unaware of your approach, and after making any unintended contact with someone.

May I: When asking permission.

Can I: When gauging ability.

Won't you: The most polite way to ask someone to do something.

Similarly, say "Would you" when making a request unless you are genuinely asking if the person is able to comply. For example "The book is on the shelf above you. Would you hand it to me?" is a polite request and has a different meaning than "The book is on the shelf above you. Could you hand it to me?" The latter asks about ability.

The sophisticated child is sensitive to adversities experienced by others, particularly if she has played a role in them, unintentionally or otherwise. In situations where your child has offended or disappointed someone or has caused an injury, accident, or unwelcome incident, she should promptly and sincerely apologize. She should begin with "I apologize" and should not leave out the reason for the apology. This helps her learn the value of being responsible and humble. A sentence beginning with "I'm sorry" is a little different as it simply conveys sympathy or empathy. Your child would apologize to her little brother for breaking his toy but she would tell her best friend she is sorry that he didn't do well on his science quiz.

Social Graces

Teach your child to use a moderate tone and volume when speaking. Whether justly or not people who speak loudly at inappropriate times are often seen as boorish or overbearing. It is also more pleasant to speak with someone who modulates her voice according to the environment she finds herself in. Even in noisier circumstances, such as at a sporting event, advise your child against attempting to speak to someone who is so far away that she must shout. Above all, enforce the habit of listening actively and respectfully in a conversation and refrain from interrupting unless it is absolutely necessary. Likewise she must use care when adjusting the volume of her devices when headphones are used. In addition to the damage loud music can do to hearing over time it is inconsiderate to force others to listen to your media just because they are sitting or standing near you.

Unless it is unavoidable, your child should not gesture for anyone at a distance to approach her, especially if the person is an adult. Such gestures will give the impression that her time and energy are more important than those of others.

It is entirely improper for her to correct the manners, speech or practices of anyone. An exception may be made if an acquaintance is actively learning a new language or customs and has expressly requested that others help him by correcting his mistakes. In this case it should be done as politely and inconspicuously as possible.

Let your child know that if she notices someone has something amiss in someone's appearance - for example, an open zipper or a particle of food stuck in the teeth - she should make the person aware of it out of the hearing of others. Similarly, she should never point at people when referring to them or make comments about people she observes in public. It is equally impolite to stare at anyone for any reason.

If she has to sneeze or cough she should do so into her forearm, as close to the armpit as possible. If she is in company and must blow her nose she should step away from the group to do so, if at all possible. Also, establish the habit of knocking before opening a closed door, even if she thinks no one is in the room. This seems silly but the point of insisting your child learn this method is to make it a practice that she will soon do as second nature.

When conversing in a group your child should make every effort to include everyone present in the conversation. If Uncle Will happened to be in the kitchen at the beginning of your discussion it is important to help him feel at ease slipping into the conversation. This can be done by making eye contact and physically creating a space for the person. There is nothing wrong with explicitly inviting someone to join in by asking them a question pertinent to a topic. Grace during this kind of situation will go a long way towards her developing a mature, inclusive communication style.

It is potentially disrespectful to reference private conversations unless given permission to do so by the relevant parties. If there is any uncertainty about this at all it is better to avoid that particular topic altogether. Your child may have enjoyed Uncle Sean's story about how he met Aunt Gabi, but it would be improper for her to recount the tale to others unless Uncle Sean is also present to approve of or discourage the idea.

It is never okay to mock, ridicule or tease anyone whether or not they are present. Even if the person in question is joining in the negative comments himself and doesn't seem to mind it is not a good habit to form. Often people who are nervous or insecure pretend to go along with jokes or comments that they secretly find hurtful. Acknowledge to your child that it takes courage and integrity go against what the crowd is doing. But the person who is the butt of the joke will know that someone took the high road. Eventually your child will earn a reputation for having integrity and for being a genuinely kind and empathetic person.

If your child is bi or multilingual teach her to refrain from speaking in a language that will not be understood by everyone in the group. When this is unavoidable she should politely ask the pardon of the others in the group before proceeding. Let's say her cousin Kayla is visiting for two weeks and your child takes her to the school dance to meet her friends. Kayla only speaks Mandarin, however, which your daughter's friends do not. Your child should inform her friends of the situation and politely ask them if she may speak Mandarin. They will gladly agree, of course and then she can freely switch between English and Mandarin for the rest of the evening. It is a formality but it shows consideration for all parties involved.

By observing you in social settings your child will learn to calibrate the tone and subject matter of her conversations to those present. With practice this will become second nature. As the appropriateness of certain subjects is dependent on the contexts, you should work with your child to help her understand the "audience."

Convey to her that it is always a good idea to direct conversations to topics that are of interest to those present. Ultimately the goal is to actively listen and show genuine interest in the lives of others.

When meeting up with someone she has not seen or spoken to in awhile, your child should try to reference something interesting from her last contact with them. Aunt Charlene will be gratified and impressed that your child asked how her hydrangea did at the flower show. It makes it evident that she was actually listening when her aunt told her about it two months before, a true mark of sophistication.

When excited about the topic being discussed, people often have a tendency to finish the sentences of the speaker. Teach your child to avoid this habit. People deserve to have the space to communicate in the manner best suited to them, which includes allowing them to share information without being interrupted. When conversing with others your child should give them her full attention and refrain from looking at her watch or cell phone. She should also avoid glancing around the room or gesturing at someone else.

Your child should also learn that people enjoy the sense of validation that comes from sharing details of their lives with others. Teach her that being a good conversation partner will sometimes mean letting others shine. If her neighbor, Isabelle, is gushing about how the cutest boy at tennis camp is interested in her, your child should not respond with the fact that the cutest boy at her school just started following her on Instagram. Connecting and empathizing with others is important, but understanding that we don't always have to be in the spotlight keeps us from crossing the line into self-absorption, a sure sign of inconsideration.

It is important for your child to send the message to others that she enjoys their company and is interested in what they have to say. Indifference and disinterest are the enemies of sophistication. If your child treats others with respect she will be pleased to find that people truly look forward to spending time with her.

Comportment

Lessons in comportment need to begin at a very early age. For example, even toddlers should start developing the habit of never putting their fingers in their mouth, nose, or ears when in public. Good posture can also be taught from a young age -- it will be directly beneficial to your child as it strengthens her core, keeps her spine well supported which minimizes the risk of neck and back pain, and makes standing and sitting for long periods of time less tiring. It gives her a more attractive appearance and connotes confidence and ease.

There are a number of simple habits your child can develop that will promote a graceful carriage and bearing. Remind her to try to keep her hips, shoulders and ears in a straight line, both while sitting or standing. The line should not be held rigidly or stiffly as this will cause fatigue. When walking, swinging her arms or walking with her head down should be avoided. These habits are unsafe and unattractive. When standing it is okay to hold one's hands in front or behind but crossing arms should be avoided. This indicates defensiveness or guardedness, and will make others feel uncomfortable or apprehensive about approaching.

Most children learn public niceties like holding the door for others or giving up one's seat. But even these simple courtesies can serve as a sign of sophistication when done properly. When holding the door for someone your child should stand to the left or right of the open door. Holding the door after one has already gone through is a kind gesture but ultimately proves to be cumbersome and awkward, especially if the person is holding bags or more than one person is entering.

An older child should relinquish her seat for any elderly person regardless of gender, as well as for any pregnant woman or anyone holding a small child. Males should always offer their seat to a female of any age if no other seats are available. Instruct your child to simply rise, gesture towards the seat and ask "Won't you sit?". This is more polite than the imperative "Please have a seat."

There is a particular way for females to enter and exit a vehicle. To enter, she should open the vehicle door and turn until she is facing the opposite direction of the seat. She should lower herself until she is fully seated. She will then turn her torso until she is facing forward while simultaneously bringing both legs, knees comfortably together, into the car. Now she may reach over and close the door. To exit she will perform the same operation in reverse. These techniques are to be used even if pants or shorts are worn.

Your child should avoid crossing the legs at the knees in public settings. Crossed legs take up space used for other people to sit, stand or walk if they are nearby, causing them to alter their movements accordingly. Crossing the legs at the ankles is fine as long as others have plenty of room to walk by.

In public arenas such as movies, theaters, concert venues, places of worship etc teach your child to make her way to and from her seat while facing the other patrons. It is considered rude to offer people a view of your bottom as you pass in front of them in such close proximity. If, at the time, your child happens to be holding or carrying large or multiple bags she should try to carry them as close to her legs as possible in order to avoid striking a passerby in the face. The opposite is true when carrying open food or drink, especially if it is hot. The person your child is passing as she makes her way by should have every opportunity to notice the potentially hot or messy food before it is uncomfortably close to their faces.

The Considerate Houseguest

There are several things your child needs to know for times when she has the good fortune to be invited to spend extended time with friends or family. If you will not be accompanying her on a visit she should always present the host or hosts with a small token of her regard. If the occasion is being hosted by a couple the momento should be presented to both, as it is common but not necessarily

20

equitable to present a gift to the female only. It should not be assumed that she did all of the work necessary for your child to have a pleasant stay just because she is a female.

Teach your child to make the same good decisions regarding behavior as you have taught her to do at home. She must take care that her grooming and hygiene are up to par and that she carefully follows any instructions regarding medications that you have given her. She should be able to properly assemble and pack her own luggage and she should always remember to carry money with her when she is away from home. Teach her to be prepared to pay for any extra items she might be interested in when she is spending the night away from home. You do not want her to be presumptuous when it comes to the finances of others. If an adult insists on purchasing something for your child when you are not there she must politely accept and thank them for the gesture.

A certain amount of cheerful chaos is expected when people have children or teens over as guests but no one likes to see their home turned into a disaster zone just because they have company. Your child should know to pick up after herself, carry her dishes and utensils into the kitchen after meals and leave the bathroom tidy and clean after each use.

Accidents do happen and should your child break or damage the property of anyone she is visiting she should notify them right away. Her willingness to be honest and upfront will almost always make a bigger impression on her hosts than the accident, itself. Instruct your child to let you know about the situation as soon as possible. This gives you the opportunity to apologize yourself and offer reimbursement if that is appropriate.

If your child needs assistance with anything or has concerns she should not hesitate to ask. For example, if she doesn't know where the towels are kept or she needs an extra blanket at night she should not be shy about making these kinds of requests. That said, there is a difference between being conscientious and being a complainer. Being disagreeable, argumentative or showing disappointment in her host's choice of food or entertainment during the stay is the epitome of ingratitude and bad form.

As we will discuss in greater detail in the chapter on communication, your child should send a handwritten note thanking her host for having her. The note should not be addressed to her friend but rather to the adult or adults in the home; in most cases, the parents of her friend. It is extra thoughtful to mention in the note any particular aspects of her stay that were especially nice. If she thought her friend's dad made the world's best pasta sauce then that would certainly be something to include.

If you consistently enforce basic courtesies with your child from a young age she should have no problems observing them while away. When children behave in a sophisticated manner when their parents are not around, it is an excellent reflection on guidance they have received.

Chapter 4
Dining Etiquette

"Dinner is not what you do in the evening before something else.
Dinner is the evening."
Art Buchwald

Good manners at mealtime makes for a more enjoyable
experience for all present. While the manifest purpose of a meal is
sustenance the stated goal is to dine, eating with friends, family and
colleagues is about so much more. "Breaking bread" is about
camaraderie, celebration and strengthening of personal and cultural
bonds.

For this reason, you should make sure your child does not
become too hungry before dining socially. A small snack beforehand
will prevent him from forgetting his manners and social
responsibilities while focussing on the satisfaction of his hunger.
This will serve especially well in situations when your child will be
dining at functions organized around very specific social goals such
as receptions, banquets, galas, charity balls and fundraisers. These
are events where it is common practice to have plated dinners and
requesting additional servings of food is considered to be impolite.

Work with your child to observe the following rules:

It is no longer necessary for males to hold the chair for
females while they are being seated at the table. If you choose to
have your child follow this charming practice make sure he
understands that it is a formality and he must not attempt to actually
maneuver the chair closer to the table once the female is seated.
Ladies should be taught to position their chair closer to the table
themselves even if a male has graciously shown her to her seat. You
should, however, teach your child that he is to remain standing until
all females who will be dining at the table are seated. It is no longer

necessary for him to stand if one of the ladies excuses herself from the table but he should stand when she returns. In addition, if a female arrives to the table for the first time at any point after the meal has begun males should stand until she is seated.

Your child should place his napkin in his lap as soon as he is seated. If he is at home or at the home of an acquaintance he should quietly retrieve his napkin if it falls from his lap. If he is dining in a restaurant he should politely ask a member of the wait staff for a new napkin. The dropped napkin should be left where it falls until a member of the waitstaff can remove it. This seems rude but the logic is sound. In a public setting it is disruptive and unsanitary to feel around under a table to locate a napkin.

Elbows should not be placed on the table before, during or after the meal although the restriction on forearms is rarely observed anymore.

Do not allow your child to single handedly bring back the aggressive middle ages by gesturing with utensils in his hand when speaking to anyone at the table.

If anyone at the table chooses to say grace or prayers before a meal teach your child to bow his head and remain quiet until the prayer is finished, even if this is not a common practice at home. He does not have to close his eyes or participate but common courtesy reminds us to respect the religious observations of others.

When dining at home or in another's home, he should not begin eating until the most senior female -- or the guest of honor at a party -- does so. This rule does not apply in restaurants or other public dining.

Your child should use his utensils as quietly as possible and refrain from making noise when placing objects on his plate or on the table. Used utensils should always be placed on the plate, never back on the table. When he when he finishes his soup, the spoon should go on the service plate located beneath the soup bowl. If there is no service plate the soup spoon should simply be placed into the empty bowl. When he is finished eating your child should place his knife and fork side-by-side along the right side of the plate near the rim. This serves as a message to wait staff, if present, that it is OK to remove the plate. If your child is not yet a coffee drinker, teach him to turn the coffee cup upside down at the beginning of the meal to indicate that he will not be having coffee when it is served after the meal.

During the meal it is not necessary for your child to remain silent. Stimulating conversation is one of the pleasures of sharing a meal with others. Encourage him to converse with those seated to his right, his left and those sitting opposite him. He must avoid raising his voice to be heard and should not attempt to speak with anyone seated more than three seats away from him unless he is being addressed directly.

He should never speak with food in his mouth. Remind him that he must wipe his mouth before he takes a drink. This prevents unsightly residue from visibly sullying the rim of his glass.

If he is served something he does not care for he should simply leave it on his plate without drawing attention to himself. You can gently suggest he try it but gatherings are not the best time to negotiate with him about his culinary likes and dislikes.

Of course, your child should always chew his food with his mouth closed. All food should be swallowed before another bite is taken and before a beverage is consumed. Taking smaller, more manageable bites makes this rule easier to observe.

If he realizes something unpleasant is in his mouth after taking a bite of food he should remove it and place it near the rim of his plate. The key is to remove the food the same way it entered. For example, if a forkful of roast beef has a bit of fat in it your child should put the fork back into his mouth, deposit the fat onto the tines of the fork and discreetly place the fat on the plate. If a spoonful of soup leaves a bit of clam shell into his mouth he should raise the spoon back to his mouth, deposit the debris onto it and place it onto the service plate beneath the soup bowl. Similarly, since fruit is eaten by hand it is perfectly fine to remove any pips, seeds or stones

25

by hand, as well. This technique minimizes the chance that other diners will notice that something unpleasant has made its way into your child's mouth. Under no circumstances should he make faces or disparaging remarks, nor should he spit the offending item into his napkin. Following these rules shows respect to everyone at the table and to those who will clean up after the meal.

If your child needs to sneeze or cough he should do so into his napkin after turning his head to the side. It is never acceptable to blow one's nose at the table. Ever.

Reaching for a platter or bowl of food is only acceptable once you have decided that your child is old enough to do so without dropping it. Even then teach him that this should only be attempted if the dish is immediately to his right, left or center. Otherwise he should ask to be served or have the dish placed within his reach.

If the meal is served buffet style teach your child to use the appropriate utensil to serve each dish. If the pasta spoon happens to be missing he should not use the salad tongs just because they are lying nearby. He should take care not to spill food or make a mess and he should never lean over a dish to get a closer look at it. If he is unsure what the dish is he should ask the closest guest or member of the wait staff. Likewise your child should never take food from the buffet with his hands, even bread rolls and he must always use a new dish when helping himself to more food.

When your child is ready to leave the table he should ask to be excused. When permission is given he should place his napkin to the right of his plate and quietly push his chair back, rise and replace his chair under the table. As he grows and mature or for an older child "May I be excused?" Becomes "Would you excuse me?" Although at any age he should have a proper understanding of his social responsibility as a member of the family. Dinner is not to be wolfed down in order to be excused and pick up where he left off in his video game domination. A reasonable amount of time is to be expected for conversation and interaction. This is doubly true if guests are present for dinner. If dining at the home of others teach your child to thank the host or hostess for the meal after he has been given permission to be excused. If he found a particular dish to be tasty or if the cook prepared something especially for him this should be acknowledged.

Lastly, we want to touch upon the importance, when eating out, of showing respect for the wait staff. These lessons should begin at home and be reinforced when you eat out with your child. Your child should have a clear understanding that rudeness towards the wait staff at an establishment reflects poorly on him and will not be allowed. When being addressed by the waiter, waitress or hostess your child should maintain eye contact and speak up so as to be heard clearly. If he is unsure of what to order he should ask the waiter for additional time to make his selection. It is impolite to assume the waiter will stand there while he reads the menu. When giving his order or requesting any items such as more water or another napkin, for instance, he should make sure he has the waiter's attention before making the request. As usual, please and thank you is essential during these exchanges.

By following the guidelines outlined in this chapter your child will soon learn and master the social skills necessary to make every dining experience an exceptionally pleasant one for himself and those around him.

Chapter 5
The Art of Communication

"A friendship can weather most things and thrive in thin soil; but it needs a little mulch of letters and phone calls and small, silly presents every so often just to save it from drying out completely."
Pam Brown

As the above quote eloquently notes, quality communication is the lifeblood of strong and rewarding relationships. In this chapter, we discuss the habits that your child will need to develop into a well-mannered communicator. Many of these habits are relevant regardless of the level of formality of the relationship or of the social context.

Correspondence

Few things are as delightful as receiving a thoughtful note or email that had not been expected. This pleasant experience is something your child can convey to others quite easily as he learns the basics of polite communication. Even for young children, correspondence only needs to be monitored enough to ensure sincerity, decorum, and the use of appropriate language. Otherwise, resist the urge to dictate or edit his thoughts or manner of expression. It is his own thoughts in his own words that the recipient of the communication will find most charming. Help him send beautiful correspondence by presenting him with a stationary set, a supply of pens, an address book, envelope seals and postage. Personalized letterhead and notecards will give that extra touch of distinction to his notes, letters and invitations.

Make expressions of gratitude and appreciation a habit for your child. Thank you notes are essential in this regard. These need not be long, but they should always be specific and sincere. For example, instead of thanking Uncle Bruce and Aunt Heather for his

28

birthday gift your child should thank them for the "amazing" telescope and inform them that he has already used it to examine a crescent moon.

Gifts are not the only reasons to send thank you notes. Anytime someone has done something for the benefit of your child -- whether this was including him in a special event, providing him assistance with a task like a school project, or holding a party or other gathering in his honor -- a thank you note is called for. It is not necessary for him to send a note following a gathering that was attended by the whole family or for one not given specifically for him.

Letters and cards are a wonderful way to keep up with family and friends who live out of town. Your child should ask the individual he is addressing about how she is doing, remembering to reference prior conversations with her or whatever positive news he has heard of her since last they spoke. He should bring his correspondents up to date on what is going on in his life including school, activities and hobbies. Little extra touches like a photo of your child engaging in one of the activities described in the letter will no doubt bring a smile to the face of an uncle in the military, or a faraway cousin.

In our modern age, handwritten notes are a particular treat to receive because of their rarity and "retro" quality. However, emails are also a convenient and effortless way to communicate with family and friends. It goes without saying that your child's email ID should be age appropriate and in good taste. When writing to an adult, texting acronyms and slang should be avoided. TTYS is no way for your child to tell his piano teacher that he will talk to him soon, even if their relationship is relaxed and casual.

We all have that email correspondent who forwards us several emails a day, all too often with admonitions to forward it to several other people in a set period of time. In spite of the questionably inspirational message of many such forwards, most people find an inbox full of them quite irritating. Make sure that your child knows that forwards should only go to friends and relatives that he is sure will appreciate them. Also, your child should be aware that forwarding a personal email or an excerpt from a personal email without the knowledge and consent of the sender is improper.

Condolence letters are a thoughtful way for your child to let others he is close to know he is thinking of them during their time of loss. They should be sent in a timely manner unless circumstances dictate otherwise.

Digital invitations have grown in popularity as people realize they can point and click their way to a party in record time. There is much to be said for the ability to issue, respond to, and access invitations without picking out stationery or making a trip to the mailbox. As the gathering is the main focus, if e-vites and group invitations online are easier for you or your child then certainly use them to let friends and family know you are ready to party. We note, however, that the pleasure of opening mail that one knows is not going to be a bill and handling the beautifully colored or textured paper cannot be equaled by online invitations. If your child does use hard copy stationary, then invitations should always be handwritten, even they are pre-printed ones. Be sure all relevant information is included and help your child keep track of responses in order to better prepare for the get together.

When your child is the recipient of an invitation, he should respond as promptly as possible. If his intention is to attend the event, he should express that he is looking forward to it if provided the opportunity to do so. If he has to decline, he should state his regrets that he will not be able to attend and send wishes that everyone has a wonderful time. It is not good form to give the reason one will not be attending unless it is done so over the phone or in person.

Get well cards should be kept as brief as possible. Your child must not use this as an opportunity to tell the person what is going on in his life. Having suffered a health setback, the recipient only needs to know that your child is wishing them a speedy recovery. Should he wish to communicate more than this a phone call is the better way to do so.

Congratulatory cards are a surefire way for your child to demonstrate that he cares about what is going on in his friends' and relatives' lives. We are apt to remember birthdays and anniversaries, but people are often particularly warmed when their accomplishments, large or small, are acknowledged. If cousin Mimi has just placed well in a dance competition a congratulatory note can be of inestimable value.

Of course, sometimes the most appreciated correspondences are those sent for no reason at all other than the desire to stay in touch and express regard. Sophisticated adults know that the most interesting people are those who are most interested. With your help, your child can develop this quality early in life and carry it with him always.

Telephone Etiquette

All of the basic rules of conversation discussed in earlier chapters also apply when speaking to someone on the telephone. However, the absence of the visual cues that one enjoys in face-to-face contact means that additional rules are needed to make telephone conversations comfortable and enjoyable for everyone.

When your child is the one making the call there are several things he should keep in mind. First, a call should never be initiated when he is out of breath, eating or otherwise indisposed. If calling a landline, your child should not assume that the person he is trying to reach is the person who has answered the telephone. He should begin the call with a greeting regardless of who answers, and ask whether the person to whom he wants to speak is available. If he is informed that the person is unavailable, your child should thank the individual on the line and ask them to please let so-and-so know that he called. If he gets the intended person on the line he should always ask whether he or she is busy or free to talk. It is frustrating to receive a phone call from someone who launches into a lengthy conversation

31

before you have a chance to tell them that you're cooking dinner or that you were just about to jump into the shower.

Your child should be encouraged to develop the habit of giving his full attention to the person with whom he is speaking on the telephone. He should not interrupt a call to speak to someone who is in the room with him unless it is absolutely necessary. It is impolite to have a stop-and-go conversation with someone. If too many distractions present themselves it may be better that he continue the call at a time when he is free to give the person his full attention. This includes using the call-waiting feature on the phone. There will be times when an important incoming call is expected and the call must be taken. If this is the case your child should politely interrupt, apologize and ask the other party if he may call them back because he has to take a call. This should only happen in extremely important situations. It will take discipline and habit but he will begin to understand that is it is rude to interrupt one phone call to take another when it is not absolutely necessary. The second caller will not be offended because he knows that when your child is on the phone with him he will be extended the same courtesy.

A three-way call should never be placed unless all parties involved are aware of the arrangement. Similarly, make sure that your child knows to never have someone on speaker unless they are aware of the fact and agree to it. This is especially important if other people are within earshot of the conversation.

There are also important habits that you should instill in your child for answering incoming calls. If he answers a phone call intended for someone else in the home, he should politely tell the caller that he will get the person for them. He should take the phone to them quietly and should never shout to notify people that they have a phone call. Also, he should refrain from revealing the identity of the caller unless he is specifically asked to do so. His father may not need to know that the caterer is on the phone for his mother and she will be glad that the surprise birthday dinner she is planning will not be spoiled.

If someone calls to speak to anyone who is unavailable at the time, your child should simply tell them so and ask if he may take a message. He should not give any additional information about the person's whereabouts or what they may be doing at the moment. Unless it is necessary or arrangements have been made beforehand your child should not call people after 9 o'clock in the evening. For the same reasons instruct your child not to call or text others during school or work hours.

The ubiquity of cellphones has dramatically increased the opportunities for young people to behave in public in ways that are less than charming. Teach your child that just because he can have a telephone conversation anywhere does not mean that he should. Your child's cell phone ringer should be on silent during social events and outings where ringing could be distraction for others – for example, at a theatre, concert venue, art gallery or restaurant. Phones set on vibrate make as much as or more noise as a ringing phone so silent mode is always the better choice. In unusual circumstances in which your child absolutely has to be available to take a call during a social occasion, the vibrate setting can be used. However, your child should know that he needs to leave the area to have his conversation.

Ringers and ring tones should be tasteful and free of profanity or inappropriate phrases or lyrics. Also, your child should never use an offensive or mocking picture ID or screen name for any of the contacts stored in his phone. The sophisticated child does not behave or express himself in ways that have the potential to hurt the feelings of others unnecessarily.

Finally, your child should return missed calls or texts as soon as it is convenient to do so. The sophisticated person extends his good manners to everyone he comes in contact with, whether in person or on the telephone.

Skillful and well-mannered communication will be an important component of your child's public presentation. The guidelines laid out in this chapter will be easier for your child to remember with practice. This will be the case for younger children, in particular, and your supervision will make all the difference early on. As with much of what we discuss in this book, the point is to gradually develop the habits of proper etiquette. By the time he reaches adulthood, skillful communication will come easily for your child, as will the benefits that come from this sophistication.

Chapter 6
Wardrobe and Grooming

"What's practical is beautiful and suitability always overrides fashion"
Billy Baldwin

We've all heard the phrase "the clothes make the man." Well this is only true if the man has no better or additional qualities to recommend him. First impressions are very important but only because they preclude others from forming hasty opinions about us that may prevent them from getting to know us better.

Can you name the haberdasheries or designer labels for the last three presidents? Chances are you cannot but you could probably state your views on their policies without much hesitation. While it is true that we can make a statement with what we wear, it is not always advisable that we do so. People with interesting and diverse outlooks on life have more valuable things to contribute than their looks alone.

Appearance becomes part of an admirable whole for people who display humor, grace and intelligence. When a person's clothing and style is consistently conspicuous or ill-suited to the occasion it becomes clear that he or she is relying on these things to do most of the talking. Sophisticated people understand this well. They know that appearance is a component of substance - not a substitution for it.

This is especially important for children to understand because often the packaging is seen as more important than the contents. Children can develop self-esteem issues associated with appearance, especially given the importance it is accorded in popular media. As a parent, however, you are in a position to help your child give the appropriate level of priority to her appearance.

Confidence should not come from knowing you look good but rather from the absence of worrying about whether or not you look good. The same is true for children. Dressing well and dressing appropriately for every occasion will free up her attention and focus, placing it instead on the individuals, events and circumstances at hand. This will help her side-step many of the issues associated with being seen as shallow or superficial.

Fashion and Style

Having said that, fashion can be fun and stimulating. Indeed, the appreciation and study of fashion as a cultural and historical mirror has all but elevated it to an art form on par with music and drama. This is a wonderful aspect of fashion to enjoy and explore with your child.

Plays, movies and period dramatic pieces are excellent ways to broaden the conversation about apparel beyond what's on the pages of the latest teen fashion magazine. What was the symbolism behind Elizabeth I's court dress? How did Audrey Hepburn's relationship with the Givenchy design house establish her as an icon of style and taste? Why is an ounce of Jean Patou's Joy such an expensive commodity? How did Coco Chanel redefine women's fashion and what affect did that have on traditional gender assumptions? How has outsourcing in the textile industry affected the price of clothing?

A child of any age can engage in meaningful, provocative dialogue about fashion. If you are fortunate enough to live in or near a large metropolitan area take advantage of the spring and fall fashion and trunk shows sponsored by department stores, fashion houses and design institutes. Again, the messages you want to impart to your child are absorbed effortlessly when they aren't even aware that they are learning.

Children tend to use clothing as a way to assert their budding independence. Your approach can keep this from becoming a source of contention and frustration between you and your child. We are not suggesting that you take a laissez-faire attitude if your child wants to wear her zebra pajamas to school - only that teaching moments come up all the time, even in times when your child is feeling less than cooperative. Finding them will be its own reward as you navigate rough waters with your little fashionista.

Let's imagine you're dressing for a dinner party and your child insists on wearing a glittery, sparkling ballet tutu instead of the $80 shantung capri pants you bought for her. You know what? Let her wear the tutu. Crushing her sense of whimsy will do nothing to cultivate a sense of style for your child. It is not necessarily a battle of wills. She is simply trying to tell you something about herself. Listen carefully and then take the lead.

Compliment her ownership of her appearance and use it as an opportunity to open the conversation about choices. Explain to her that she can wear the sparkly tutu but she should understand that it is not the most appropriate thing in her closet to consider. Tell her that in this is a situation where there is room for negotiation, but also that this will not always be the case. Then unveil some awesome ideas to add to the fun.

You can show her how to further explore the topic of ballet and ballet costumes. She can read age-appropriate books on ballet and describe her favorite parts to you; watch documentaries on or video clips about actual child ballerinas; recreate a scene from Tchaikovsky's Swan Lake with her dolls or arts and crafts supplies. Introduce her to basic French ballet terms such as pas de deux or pliè and see if she can reproduce the first five positions. Kick off your shoes and do it with her! In future she will don her tutu with pride because she not only earned it but because her appreciation is now informed.

More importantly, you have quieted her frustration - not her voice - and created a platform for growth and development. With time she will find more constructive, cooperative ways to display her individuality and creativity because you wisely chose to not make her behavior the basis for your response.

Whether your child is a primary schooler or a high schooler there are ways to promote autonomy and maturity when it comes to building her wardrobe. Begin by giving her a clothing allowance that is age appropriate and not overly generous. The extra money will inevitably lead to some impulsive buys. Encourage her to create a shopping list based on what she needs or thinks she might like to purchase.

With her budget already determined this allows her to see for herself whether or not the list is reasonable or needs to be trimmed. After she completes her list (you will want to review it if your child is younger) wait several days before taking her to make her purchases. Chances are she will not want some items as much as she originally thought she did.

Discourage her from putting together outfits. This leads to an accumulation of trendy pieces in her wardrobe that only work together as opposed to becoming wardrobe essentials that pair well with everything and stand the test of time. When shopping set aside all or most of the day so there is no rushing around, grabbing unnecessary items out of expedience or fatigue.

As much as possible take your child to stand-alone shops and boutiques. This way there is little distraction or enticement from more trendy stores with poorer quality clothing. When mall or outlet shopping is inevitable encourage her to examine the quality and workmanship of the items she is considering. Compare and contrast items of differing quality and point out the subtle variations that you find. Is the fabric content appropriate to the use of the garment? Do the hems, plackets and button holes lie flat? Is single or double stitching used? Is the fabric dyed or has the garment itself been dyed? Is there puckering at seam lines?

Eventually she will get a sense of what labels provide consistent quality and will become her go to as she ages. It is never too early to introduce your child to good tailoring or bespoke clothing and accessories. Take her to a seamstress or local designer and have her off the rack clothes tailored or let her commission a custom dress or a one of a kind accessory such as a headband or hand-knitted scarf. She will learn to appreciate the artistry and skill involved in the process and your obvious pleasure in the results will resonate with her in her future choices.

These steps may not always dissuade her from making a purchase you consider regrettable and that's okay. We want to win the war, not necessarily every little battle! Over time you will see your patience and consistency pay off. Cringe-worthy jeans and band tour schedule t-shirts are going to make their way into your child's wardrobe but the day will come when you hear your teen sigh in frustration because an item she wants has a high polyester content, poorly aligned buttonholes or an uneven hemline.

You won't say anything but you will think back to this chapter and smile from ear to ear. At that point we strongly encourage you to give yourself a small but meaningful pat on the back.

Give your child a certain amount of responsibility for the care and maintenance of her wardrobe. You may not want her to do her own laundry on a regular basis but she should at least learn how. She will be at a distinct advantage in this department when she goes off to summer camp, studies abroad or heads off to college. The sophisticated child is not helpless! Caring for her wardrobe will give her added wear and ensure she always looks her best. For example, the beautiful leather boots she is so proud of will keep their appeal and durability if she remembers to clean them and stuff them with butcher paper before storing them away for spring. Another example would be for you to teach her that sweaters should be removed by pulling them over the head by the waistband as opposed to the arms in order to maintain the proper shape and prevent sagging.

Wardrobe

Although your child has a unique personal style it is important that she have the appropriate clothes for every occasion.

The following categories will give you a helpful overview of the wardrobe building process and prevent you from packing your child's closet with cute but eventually redundant and pointless items.

School Clothes -- If your child wears a uniform you have most of your work done for you. Make sure items are fitted properly and are kept clean and in good repair. If her school doesn't require a uniform understand that the principle concerning uniforms still applies. The focus should be on academics and not on apparel. Allow her to express her individuality and style through her accessories. Funky hair ties or a colorful backpack will keep her from becoming bored with her look, without making her a slave to ever changing trends and fads.

Weekend or Casual Wear -- Your child may have a lot more leeway in this category. Time spent with friends or socializing is a great time for your child's own style to take center stage. Within the limits of decorum let her wear clothes that make her feel beautiful or edgy, sporty or cool, literal or ironic - this is when it is okay for her to have fun with fashion.

Semi-formal Wear -- Religious gatherings, dinner at Grandma's, attending a sibling's recital - these are examples of occasions that call for semi-formal attire. She may prefer to go to Grandma Janice's in slouchy jeans and a comfortable hoodie but your goal is to set the bar higher. It will become second nature for your child to meet and even exceed your expectations when you, yourself, are unwavering about them. Explain to her how important it is to show respect for events and for those with whom we choose to spend time, even if grandma could care in the least! Your child will be less likely to balk at wearing her best jeans and a nice sweater to visit relatives or to attend a social event once she understands the importance of being appropriate. It is also a good idea to for your child to wear items she received as a gift from the person being visited.

Formal Wear -- Your child's formal wear should be of good quality and fit, as special occasion clothing looks much worse than casual clothing when they are poorly made, lack proper fit or seem otherwise cheap.

Sleepwear and Intimates -- Comfort is key. Natural fibers are more breathable and have a softer hand, keeping your child cool in warmer months and warm when the temperature drops. Flame retardant sleepwear is a good option as long as your child has shown no previous skin reaction to the material.

Footwear -- Buying well-made footwear is rarely a cheap endeavor, especially during ages when your child seems to go up half a shoe size every six months. Nevertheless providing her with well-constructed footwear is essential to her comfort and the support of her feet, legs and core. Shoes that are too small, too large, too narrow or too wide affect not only comfort and mobility but posture as well. During her periods of rapid growth, take her for regular fittings, preferably in the evening when her feet will be at their most expansive. Although fitting stockings are provided by merchants always make sure your child tries on shoes with the socks or hosiery she will actually be wearing with that particular shoe. For example dress socks or tights with dress shoes and athletic socks with tennis shoes and sneakers. If she uses a public pool or shower insist that she wear rubber or plastic sandals, perforated garden clogs or thongs at all times until she is ready to put her street shoes back on.

Accessories -- This is where your child can have a little fun. A scarf in a bright color or vivid pattern, gloves in an unusual hue, silly socks or a funky, fringed bag are all harmless and interesting ways for her to express herself. Give your child the responsibility of carrying a wallet or small handbag. Cross body bags work best for children and teens because it is much more difficult to misplace or forget than a traditional one shoulder bag or purse.

Outerwear -- Like formalwear, outerwear is another category of clothing for which skimping on quality is never a good idea. The material, drape and fit of your child's sweaters, jackets and coats are very much essential to their function. A coat that is attractive but made of cheap fabric and with arms that are too long or too short will do very little to keep the elements from affecting your child.

In transitional weather months ensure that your child has adequate layers in order to handle whatever the day's weather may bring. Outerwear in classic colors and a traditional cut work very well from season to season. Add interest and freshen the look with inexpensive, novelty accessories such as colorful scarves, gloves and umbrellas.

Grooming and Hygiene

The importance of good grooming and hygiene cannot be overstated. It is important for not only positive social interactions but physical comfort and health as well. Giving offense because of inadequate hygiene is a faux pas that is easily avoided with minimal maintenance and personal upkeep.

Teach your child the fundamentals of good grooming and hygiene and patiently reinforce them as much as is necessary. For younger children, introduction to the concepts of personal grooming and self-care can be easily done with toys and teaching aids. If your child enjoys playing with a doll observe her as she pretends to brush its teeth or comb its hair. Is she holding the brush properly? Are the fundamentals of her technique sound? Is she showing interest in doing things for herself or is she hesitant? As you help your smaller child with these tasks, do so in front of a mirror and with verbal narration, when possible. She will do things independently much sooner because of the behaviors you have modelled for her.

Take your cues from what you see. Gradually hand the reins over to your child, giving her an opportunity to put your instructions and example into use on her own. She will absorb the lessons more thoroughly this way.

Bathing -- Daily cleansing is a must, especially during the post-pubescent years. Introduce your child to fragrant bath gels, bath bombes and salts, and other ancillary products that will add a touch of luxury and enjoyment to the process. Consider bath and shower products marketed especially for children and teens - they will enjoy using a line of products designed just for them. Try your hand at making all natural soaps with your child - a particularly good idea if she has skin allergies. And what better way for her to show her creativity, originality and generosity than presenting a friend or family member with a bar of hand-milled, decadently emollient soap she made herself?

Loofahs, sea sponges and exfoliating brushes are another way to help your child enjoy her bath. These extras will encourage her to see bath time as not only a necessity but a time to relax and pamper herself after a long day. Once she is old enough to bathe unattended allow her that space to make her grooming time her own.

Oral Hygiene -- A beautiful, healthy smile truly is your best accessory and oral hygiene is another key component of good grooming. Aside from biannual trips to the dentist, children with braces or other orthodontic appliances must rinse and brush after each meal or snack. Dental floss and dental picks are an excellent way to help fight cavities, plaque, tartar buildup and bad breath. Do not assume that your child knows how to brush and floss properly. Ask your hygienist to demonstrate best practices for your child on your next visit to the dentist.

Hair, Skin and Nails -- It is important to teach your child from a very young age to care for her hair. Whether or not she washes it daily, every other day, or weekly will vary according to hair texture and family practices and preference. Make sure she has the right implements, shampoos, conditioners, detanglers, oils, creams and styling products necessary for her keep her hair clean, attractive and healthy. Testing various products in order to find what will give optimal results is important but do not experiment needlessly as this can lead to unintentional damage and product build-up.

Skincare should be a relatively simple part of your child's daily regimen. She should wash her face every morning and before bedtime whether she takes her bath or shower at that time or not. For most children a moist face cloth will suffice and no moisturizer is necessary. On special occasions, like a sleepover or a family spa night, you might make fruit puree facials with her - a fun and instructive foray into the world of luxury grooming. If eczema, rosacea, acne or any other skin condition exists always consult your child's pediatrician or dermatologist before using or discontinuing any skin care products.

Make sure your child knows that sunscreen is non-negotiable when going out in the sun. Determine which level of SPF is appropriate for her skin. In extremely hot weather or during heat advisory days encourage the use of a brimmed hat or cap as well. Reducing the risk of sun related skin cancer is your goal but youthful, more attractive skin is not a bad incentive to protect one's skin either.

There are very few circumstances when the daily use of nail polish looks appropriate on children under the age of 16. French and American natural manicures are the exception for children between the ages of 13 and 16 although many schools prohibit it altogether. For teens of this age, subtle manicures in shades of peach, pink, nude or buff are appropriate for special occasions. For teens over the age of 16 nail polish of any color can be worn for any occasion although it is not necessarily in good taste to wear vibrant colors to school, work or community activities. Your daughter may fail to make a desirable impression if she chooses to wear cherry red nail polish to help serve meals to the homeless.

Makeup -- When it comes to makeup each parent has her own rules about when it is okay for her child to begin experimenting with and wearing it. Unlike nail polish this is not as proscribed by age and can be determined based on individual factors. One parent may not even consider allowing her child to wear makeup on a daily basis until she is old enough to drive whereas another may feel that a bit of mascara and gloss will help her young teen feel better about herself and, literally, face the world. A full face of makeup, however, should rarely be worn by any child of any age. Once you and your child agree that it is time to start wearing makeup, insist on moderation.

Even for adults makeup should rarely be about a 'look' except for specific occasions. Makeup should be used to balance imperfections or to highlight one's natural beauty and best features. Teach your child that for every day wear, makeup should enhance, not alter.

To this end it is a good idea to educate your child in the purchase and application of makeup. Although there is a wealth of information online and in magazines and beauty books, the best approach begins with a trip to your local department store, salon or spa to speak to a licensed cosmetologist or aesthetician. This will give your child access to individualized advice and will also serve as a memorable, milestone on her road to adulthood. Expert tips and techniques will make you and your child more comfortable about the process and the experts are always more than happy to share their knowledge with young, future customers! Your child should adopt the belief that cosmetics should be of the highest quality one can afford, recognizing that this does not always mean the most expensive choice.

Teach your child to keep her cosmetic supplies and applicators in an organized manner and free from dust and exposure. Sharing makeup with siblings or friends is fine but disposable wedges, cotton swabs and applicators should always be used to minimize the risk of spreading any infections. Your child should wash her makeup brushes and sponges often and replace every six months or sooner, depending on use.

Jewelry -- Jewelry should be discreet and tasteful. Discrete and tasteful, of course, is in the eye of the beholder, so this is another area where family preferences will play a strong role. In general, however, children should only wear jewelry on special occasions. The exceptions include watches, inconspicuous earrings and any religious or sentimental jewelry, worn discreetly. Diamonds on children under the age of 18 is generally considered inappropriate.

The only exception is for formal events held after 6 p.m. In this context, teens may wear diamonds with the same rules of discretion being applied.

At some point your child will want to wear makeup or jewelry that you consider inappropriate for her age. She will protest that everyone else's mom lets them do it and there may be tears and slammed bedroom doors. (We assume that the crying and door slamming is done by your child and not by you.) When she is ready to listen explain to her that you want her to wait until a certain age to do some things because you have decided that is best for her appearance and priorities. Tell her how attractive you know she will be when the time comes for her to take her look to the next level but in the meantime you would be happy to help her find other ways to perk up her "look". A new haircut or fun accessory will give her something else to focus on and send her the message that she is still a partner in decisions that affect her - just not an equal one.

In this chapter, we have covered the basics of appearance, including grooming and hygiene, wardrobe essentials, and makeup and accessories. These are more than just the components of a well-dressed and cared for child. They are also perfect areas for her to demonstrate the subtle, understated elegance of a young sophisticate.

Chapter 7
The Cultivated Palate

"The art of the cuisine, when fully mastered, is the only human capability of which only good things can be said."
Friedrich Durenmatt

Food is a wonderful part of our lives in ways both great and small; a look through the culinary section of any book retailer will testify to this fact. The purpose of this chapter is to inspire you to approach cuisine in a different way with your child. Learning about food, creating amazing meals and sharing them with family and friends will be its own incentive to develop your child's palate. He will understand how using the best ingredients and taking the time and care to prepare food properly makes for the best meals. He will learn that an appreciation of cultural expression through food can add richness and enjoyment to his life.

Children are known to be picky eaters, especially when very young. Even older children have the reputation of only wanting burgers and pizza, when given a choice in the matter. This does not have to be the case. Of course, individuals will always have a natural preference for certain flavors or textures when it comes to food. However, the foods to which we are exposed have a great influence upon the foods we come to enjoy.

In France very young children are given cheeses such as Camembert, Gruyère and Roquefort before their afternoon and evening meals. They have several, simple courses at dinner and a kid's menu is relatively unheard of in French restaurants and cafes. Are French children naturally more sophisticated than other children? Not in the least; their parents simply cultivate their palate at a much younger age. Your child's taste in food and drink can be as well developed and varied as are other areas of interest in his life.

We are not going to preach against the evils of fast food or processed food items. In fact, telling your child how bad junk food is may have an effect opposite to what you desire. He will see it as something wonderful and unattainable. Nothing tempts like forbidden fruit. And, of course, it is not just your child. On a Friday night after a long week, pizza delivery can feel like a heavenly gift and who can say no to the occasional box of doughnuts? Believe us, we get it! But we are also quite certain that if you investment the time to expose your child to a variety of delicious food prepared with fresh ingredients, it will pay off handsomely in the long run.

It has been our experience that children who are regularly exposed to quality food still enjoy the fare at the local burger joint … but they do not prefer it. Similarly, a child who has limited access to carbonated and sweetened beverages may occasionally partake of them when given the opportunity. But he will not do so frequently; it is not his habit and the drinks will seem uncomfortably sweet in larger amounts. This is where your diligence pays off.

As noted, younger children can be finicky. A firm "no" or a vigorous shake of the head from them often follows a parent's attempt to get the child to try something new or, on some days, to even eat anything at all. This is normal. Toddlers have not developed the same amount of taste buds as older children and they simply do not have the same experience as adults when they taste certain foods. In addition, their growing independent streak can make even simple daily tasks a reason for tantrums, meltdowns and scenes.

This is just your child testing his boundaries and figuring out his likes and dislikes as he learns to negotiate in a world with other people in it. He is developing a sense of autonomy and wants to claim ownership of his experiences. This may extend to his meals and may explain some of his aversion to things you offer him to eat. Patience and understanding will make this process easier for both you and your little picky eater.

Introduce new foods early and often. Today's "no" will eventually become tomorrow's "yes". Tell your child that if he takes a little bite and he does not like it you will not require him to do more than that. By doing this he will come to realize that he has nothing to lose by trying the item. It is important when offering new foods to children make sure they are prepared in a manner that is safe for their developmental stage. A diced apple poses a choking hazard to toddlers so apple strips or applesauce would be a better choice.

Offer foods that your child has previously avoided in a new way. A serving of matchstick carrots accompanied with a ranch dipping sauce may make him forget about the steamed carrots he does not care much for. If he still insists on eating mashed potatoes three days in a row then let him. In this way you will have deprived him of the opportunity to stand his ground; eventually, he will grow tired of mashed potatoes. If you become concerned that he is not getting adequate nutrition, talk to your pediatrician about the issue and find a multivitamin that appeals to little taste buds.

When you discover foods that your child enjoys find different versions of the same item for him to try. For example, if he likes dumplings he may very well enjoy wonton, gnocchi or samosas. Does he love turnovers? Then try introducing him to rugelach or strudel. Gauge his tolerance for spice and or heat when it comes to introducing him to new cuisine, but for the most part, novelty is incentive enough for more adventurous children to take on the challenge of exciting new cuisine.

Again, we go back to one of the book's most important themes: exposing your child to new things. Food is one of the most enjoyable facets of sophistication; what better gift to give your child than a love of trying new and wonderful types of cuisine?

Let your child spend time with you in the kitchen as you prepare meals and snacks. Younger children will be a little less suspicious of new dishes if they see what items are being used. Give them small tasks such as helping to remove the packaging from food, lining up the spice jars, helping to wash the vegetables etc. With the exception of tasks involving heat or sharpened objects the hand-over-hand method is excellent for showing small children the best way to do basic things in the kitchen.

Involvement with meal prep is beneficial for children of all ages and can serve as an opportunity for family bonding. As long as you are comfortable with your older child's knowledge of kitchen safety, give him important roles to play while cooking. As he masters a technique, such as cracking eggs into a bowl without eggshell pieces, acknowledge the accomplishment and graduate him to a more complicated task like separating the yolk from the white. This will give him a sense of gratification and keep him engaged in the cooking experience.

While cooking with your child use the time to further educate him about cooking and cuisine. If you use proper cooking terms, your child will become familiar with culinary vernacular. Do not ask him to cut the bell pepper into thin strips for the stir-fry, ask him to julienne the bell pepper instead. If he asks you why you put the steamed green beans into ice water tell him you are shocking them to stop the cooking process in order to preserve their texture and color.

Time spent cooking with your child is also an excellent time to casually review dining etiquette do's and dont's. Teach him the proper way to set the table, explaining any placement that prompts questions from him. For smaller children, paper cut outs of dishes and utensils allow them to practice without endangering your better dishes.

Speaking of dishes, do not wait for special occasions to use your best china, flatware, stemware, serving ware or linens. The sophisticated diner is one who is comfortable with fine things and is sure of their correct usage. Identify each item as you help your child set the table, sharing with him how you came to own each piece and any other fond memories attached to your possession of it. Someday it will mean a great deal to him to entertain with the silver platter his grandmother gave you the day he came home from the hospital.

As much as is possible, make it a practice to eat meals at consistent times. This continuity creates a sense of stability in your child's life and he will come to look forward to mealtimes as an enjoyable time with family. To this end, set the expectation that books, cell phones and homework will not be brought to the table during meals.

Augment the dining experience by borrowing elements of style from your favorite restaurants. There is no reason why meals at home cannot be as relaxing and enjoyable as those eaten out. Dimmed lighting promotes a calming effect and your child can help you select instrumental music such as classical, jazz or world music to softly play in the background during the meal.

Make your child a partner in the cooking experience by showing him how you plan meals. As he begins to understand let him make menu suggestions and grocery shopping lists. As you shop for groceries he will have a more complete understanding of how and why you purchase the items you do. Show him a package of pre-made macaroni and cheese. Read the list of ingredients and the nutritional data and note the price. Next, locate each ingredient that would be used to make macaroni and cheese from scratch. What are the differences in price and nutrition? Ask your child about the comparative benefits of pre-packaged versus homemade macaroni and cheese and why might shoppers prefer one or the other.

Familiarize your child with dinner courses by picking several nights a week to serve more than one course. A typical eight course meal, used for special occasions, consists of the following, served in order, hor d'oeuvres soup, fish, sorbet, salad, main course, cheese and dessert. Your selections certainly do not have to be complicated. Even chicken noodle soup, a tuna salad sandwich, and wedges of brie can be served separately and in the proper order.

Promote his exploration of flavor by packing interesting lunches for him. There is nothing wrong with peanut butter and jelly sandwiches, for sure, but it takes no more time to prepare a Swiss and prosciutto sandwich on a sliced baguette.

Ask him questions about food that will make him think about the topic in new ways. For example, if he enjoys a particular dish at a restaurant, cook it with him at home. Let him taste the ingredients individually so he will get a sense of what exactly gives the dish its distinctive taste and overall appeal. Encourage him to read cookbooks and culinary magazines. Discuss with him how the publications use both food and decor to stage the photos in a way that says more to the reader than how to prepare a certain dish.

For which foods are your city, state or region known? North Carolina barbecue, Chicago deep dish pizza, Louisiana gumbo and New England clam chowder are a few classic examples of local cuisine rarely equaled elsewhere. Identify which foods make the cut and help your child cook up some tasty local fare.

Identify foods that have a special significance to your family's ethnic, religious or cultural makeup. Discuss the importance of these foods with your child and explain their role in any memories you associate with them from your childhood. Did your father learn to make a special challah loaf from his father? Does the smell of fresh cilantro remind you of wonderful Cinco de Mayo celebratory dinners from your childhood? Or perhaps you have a jerk chicken or bibimbap recipe that's been in your family longer than you have! Record the recipes with your child and help him learn to create and serve these important dishes.

Start a family cookbook with your child. He can help you gather your family's best recipes, interview family members about their favorite food memories and take photos to be featured in the book.

Encourage your child to give homemade treats as tokens of his regard instead of store-bought gifts. If he enjoys baking, a batch of his tempting lemon ginger biscotti is bound to put a smile on anyone's face. He should package the biscotti in a nice tin or gift bag and tuck a copy of the recipe in among the goodies.

Teach your child how to plan a picnic or tailgating party. This will give him a chance to learn how to properly prepare and pack foods, beverages and utensils that will be used away from home. Once he has the hang of it, see if he can plan a picnic for four without your assistance. Emphasize that the menu need not be complicated. Fresh breads, cheeses, cured meats such as hard salami, olives, fresh fruits and simple pastries are examples of picnic fare that is both light and pleasing.

A search for outstanding food is a great motivation for getting out into the community. Be sure to take advantage of any cultural festivals in your town. They are a perfect opportunities to introduce your child to new foods from all over the world. Teach him to pay attention to the particular flavors present in certain types of international cuisine. Perhaps this observation can serve as entry to a discussion of the agriculture and climate of region from which the cuisine originated. Farmers markets are also a fun and educational way to introduce your child to the benefits of healthy eating, of supporting local merchants and of organic, farm-to-table dining.

Do not omit gourmet and five star restaurants from your child's culinary education. Plan a special visit to a restaurant in your city known for its excellent cuisine. If you live in a large city it should be possible to find out who the executive chef is and where he studied. Sharing this information with your child will get him excited about the experience. He will pay more attention to every detail of the evening, giving him an appreciation of the art and skill of haute cuisine. Ask your child what differences he notices in the experience compared to other establishments where he has dined. Ask him what he is enjoying the most. The cuisine? The decor and ambiance? The presentation? This will not only improve his vocabulary but give him dimensions with which to describe his dining experience. He will begin to understand that food is about so much more than a meal, and his appreciation for the culinary arts will be enhanced.

Register your child for a kid's cooking class in the area. Schools, restaurants and even major food chains occasionally offer courses and workshops designed to educate and stimulate budding chefs and foodies. This environment will reinforce the things you have been teaching him at home and he will have a lot of fun connecting the dots between food, fun and fellowship. If possible, you might arrange to take your child to a live taping of a cooking show. It will be a unique experience as he gets a behind-the-scenes glimpse into the entertainment side of cooking.

In this chapter we have described ways to help your child appreciate well-prepared food, ways to introduce your child to international cuisine, and ways to expose him to the culinary arts. You do not need to try all of the ideas we have presented. But if you try at least some of them, you child will be much more likely to develop a discerning palate. And he will undoubtedly come to appreciate the limitless variety of flavors that the foods of the world can offer.

Chapter 8
The Joy of Learning

*"Tell me and I will forget, show me and I may remember, involve me
and I will understand."*
Chinese Proverb

In this chapter we will discuss your child's education. By this
we don't explicitly mean the material or subjects she will study at
school. Rather, we are referring to the total experience of life
learning and the acquisition of knowledge that begins from day one
and, hopefully, continues throughout one's lifetime. If no other
topics were covered in this book this one would still exemplify our
unchanging approach to raising a sophisticated child. The child who
has been taught to love the process of growing, learning and taking
on new challenges and experiences can face life with confidence and
poise. The parents who understand this are already ten steps ahead in
helping their child achieve this particular brand of success.

Our approach to learning is a holistic one. If straight A's are
your goal as a parent, there are great resources out there that address
achievement in academics better than we ever could. But we do
concede that the techniques discussed in this chapter also happen to
be those employed successfully by students who earn excellent
grades, although that is not our agenda, per se.

Instead, we want to help you amplify and enhance the
knowledge your child gains from her studies at school. You can
begin on this road by sharing positive aspects of your own learning
experiences, thereby allowing her to anticipate what lies in store.
The accent here is on the positive. Recounting how you were stuffed
into lockers as a freshman or how much you hated biology may be
honest, but it unlikely to make your eighth grader look forward to

entering high school. Don't hide the negative, but don't overemphasize it either.

Treat each learning milestone as an impressive rite of passage and remind your child that she has earned these achievements. If she learns how to properly cite her references on a term paper, for instance, that is an accomplishment worth noting, regardless of the grade she receives. We are not advocating that you praise mediocrity or lower the bar for your child; we are saying that acknowledging her accomplishments acts to highlight the importance of learning. She will come to see each accomplishment as a step forward on the road to the bright, knowledgeable person that she wants to become.

Remind her to show particular respect and courtesy to her instructors, faculty and staff at school. Explain that you understand that children will sometimes feel it is cool to mock or disobey authority figures but that you will not condone this behavior under any circumstances. Tell her that you have no doubt that she will do the right thing and treat others as she would like to be treated. A child who is courteous to everyone from the principal or headmaster to the custodians will be admired and respected in her own right. Refrain from disparaging your child's teachers in her hearing. Children do not always possess the appropriate filters when it comes to criticism and a lack of understanding or context may make them feel anxious or conflicted.

It is important to always look ahead as your child advances in her academic career. Make the effort to be aware of what will be covered in her history class and what books her English class will be reading in the coming year. This will not only help you to be involved in her learning, it will also model for your child the importance of preparation. Also, keep in mind possible next steps for learning outside of the classroom. What are the skills and proficiencies will be the groundwork for her next round of achievements. Focus on those qualities society looks for in a person that are not purely academic -- good character, people skills, leadership ability etc. Share with your child your aspirations for her in these areas and why who think these things are important. If she is a partner in her personal growth she will understand and more readily cooperate with the steps necessary to achieve it. Allow her to advocate for and see her own role in her success.

Many parents rightfully tell their children how proud they are of them when they accomplish a goal. This is important feedback but it is also just as beneficial to tell children that they should really be proud of themselves. As they mature they will then be less likely to look to others for approval and validation. This will not make them arrogant. Rather, they will have a healthy sense of independence and inner strength knowing that they are capable of reaching their goals. Confidence really yields results!

Most of us can agree that there are many topics of discussion that are inappropriate or downright off-limits for children. But all too often parents assume that there are things children simply aren't interested in because they do not pertain to them. This mindset robs you of chances to expose your child to a multitude of ideas, concepts and knowledge that she would otherwise be unaware of for several more years. You might be surprised how well she pays attention to your explanation of why you think the car mechanic's quote is ridiculous or why you think your colorist can't seem to find the right shade of espresso for your hair. She will understand more of what you're saying than you might imagine and she will ask you to explain the rest. These kinds of interaction are often the coal that becomes the future diamonds of sophistication!

We have all encountered children who are able to understand and, in turn, articulate concepts much differently and more effectively than do their peers. It is always fascinating when you observe a small child engaged in a coherent, nuanced conversation with adults. "How did this come about?" we ask ourselves, amazed. Well, as a parent, you can play a large role in developing these same skills in your own child. From a young age make a practice of speaking intelligently to her. There is nothing wrong with baby talk but as she emerges from toddlerhood she is cognitively and socially primed to learn and retain a great deal of information at an alarming rate. It is up to you to provide her with it.

Use words and phrases that will broaden her vocabulary over time. The only difference between the child who asks her mother not to procrastinate and the child who begs her mother to stop wasting time is their exposure to an extended vocabulary. There is nothing about their capacity to learn new words that is bound by age. It all boils down to exposure, repetition and the actual, physical context in which the words are used. In both scenarios above, the children have made themselves perfectly understood to their mothers. But the second child will be at a disadvantage if she hears the word 'procrastinate' used in conversation whereas the first child will understand exactly what is meant when she hears the word being used. This is why reading aloud to small children is recommended - the more they hear, the more they understand and can express in return.

Again, exposure is the key and that's where you, as parent, come in. When introducing a new word or phrase insert the simpler meaning or translation into the sentence for the first few times. For example, ask your child "What does the meteorologist, the weatherman on television, say about today's weather?" Eventually leave out the explanation altogether and soon you will see that your child has learned the new word completely.

With consistency and repetition children are able to learn far more than they are often given credit for. When reading aloud to a younger child, or discussing books or drama with an older child, frame the conversation in terms of antagonist, protagonist, setting, climax, resolution, point-of-view etc. In addition, do not waste any opportunity to insert vernacular or shop talk into any relevant discussions you have with your child. Use of foreign phrases, idioms and figures of speech are also excellent ways to broaden her grasp of language. Ask her if she would like a baker's dozen of valentine cookies to give to her friends after school. Tell her that she needs to abide by the de facto house rules about good table manners or tell her how your committee meeting seemed to go on ad infinitum. She will ask you what you mean and that opens the door for broadening your child's horizons even more. So give her an age appropriate definition of what a committee meeting is and explain why you were in attendance. Context plays a role in comprehension. Eventually, she will more than understand; she will begin to use complex words and phrases in everyday conversation.

Show her how to take advantage of any opportunities her school offers for growth and personal development. Clubs, workshops, immersion camps, student government and after school activities can be fun, informative and character building. If she has a particular interest not represented at her school assist her in sketching a proposal for it to be submitted to her school's activities coordinator. She will gain valuable insight into how to advocate for what she wants in life and the procedures through which she can affect change.

This is also an excellent period in your child's life to consider foreign study. Sessions can range from a term, a quarter, a semester or a full year. Shorter summer sessions are also an option. Few academic opportunities can rival study abroad when it comes to giving your child exposure to other languages, cultures and customs. If studying abroad is not a viable option for her then consider sponsoring a foreign exchange student. Again, your child will benefit immensely from living with and learning from someone her own age who comes from a different background. Take advantage of school field trips whenever possible and encourage your child to share her impressions of the experience with you.

Although we have been emphasizing learning in a variety of contexts, it is important to support your child in her scholastic endeavors. A clean, ordered study environment in key. This is another area in which to encourage independence in your child. Neatness, preparedness and organization are difficult skills for many kids to master. If your child is one of those kids who is not naturally fastidious then you have a bit more work to do teaching her the value of being tidy. Demanding or expecting perfection will only add stress to your life and to hers but setting expectations is certainly recommended.

School supplies should be stored where the child can access them independently and she should be encouraged to notify you when she is running low on a particular item. Autonomy and accountability at work, anyone?

A no food and drink policy should be implemented in her bedroom in general and in any designated study area in particular. If she is hungry she should have a snack before she starts her homework. Assignments dotted with stains or crumbs will not leave a favorable impression with your child's teacher and may not be accepted at all if she feels it displays a total lack of effort or care.

Children occasionally do poorly on an assignment simply because they lose track of when it is due or what the directions were. This can easily be avoided by teaching your child to maintain an academic agenda. Provide her with a ledger or a large blotter or wall-mounted calendar. Advise her on the best way to keep track of upcoming assignments by dedicating one day per week to filling in and updating her calendar. If her teachers hand out a syllabus or project rubric at the beginning of each semester, this will make her task that much easier. She may be several years or even more than a decade away from college but it is never too early to teach her time management and independent living skills.

As she gets the hang of keeping up with future assignments, expand the concept by letting her keep up with her own extracurricular activities, social engagements and appointments. You will be a proud parent, indeed, when your daughter reminds you that she can't go shopping for a new jacket after school on Thursday because she has an appointment with the optometrist that afternoon at 4 o'clock.

An effective way to enhance your child's formal education is to help her make relevant connections between her studies and the world at large. Once this becomes a habit for you and your child, there will be countless opportunities to explore new topics with her. Economics and math can make more sense as you and your child go shopping or make a trip to the supermarket. Socioeconomics and history can become part of the conversation after seeing a great movie. How does the principle of supply and demand affect the price of apples compared to that of imported truffle oil? What are the historical and global implications behind the types of people who tend to be represented as villains in film? How accurate or fair are these portrayals? What scientific discoveries led to the development of smartphones?

The answers to these queries are not nearly as important as the opportunities they present for your child to connect what she is learning in school to activities in the real world. You can anticipate that this will enhance her general curiosity and strengthen her ability to analyze information critically. Discuss her studies with her during down times like while traveling in the car or during mealtimes. Refrain from using these moments to focus on her grades as this should be a time for invigorating, meaningful conversation and not necessarily advice or criticism.

Learning outside of the classroom can be an exciting and productive way to spend quality time with your child and make her academic involvement more meaningful. Local colleges and universities offer a wealth of opportunity to further educate her and immerse her in an environment charged with academic exploration and curiosity. Lectures, symposiums, forums, exhibitions and recitals are often open to the general public. The subject matter can range from robotics to Commedia dell'Arte performances but the novelty of the experience will resonate with her and capture her interest even if some of the information seems to go over her head. You might also be surprised at the number of artists, teachers, instructors and professionals who would gladly set aside time in their schedule to speak with your child about their area of expertise and her interests.

And because all of this occurs outside of the classroom she will feel free to let it capture her interest without worrying about a test, quiz or written assignment to gauge her comprehension. This is the very epitome of a love of learning.

Chapter 9
Culture and the Arts

"I found that dance, music and literature is how I made sense of the world...it pushed me to think of things bigger than life's daily routines...to think beyond what is immediate or convenient."
Mikhail Baryshnikov

If you can cultivate a love of the arts in your child, you will have given her the gifts of culture, class and sophistication. When she triumphs over adversity, experiences heartache, deals with loss or discovers something that fills her with joy, she will find her story reflected in some of the world's greatest music, literature, drama and visual arts.

Whether she is swept up in a thrilling novel or arranging an original piece for a school performance, she will be intuitively building upon the culture to which she has been exposed. An appreciation of culture and the arts encourages critical thinking, delights the mind and the senses, and helps contextualize our perceptions of the world. Sophistication in these areas will be as noteworthy and admirable in your child as any of the qualities she may have absorbed in other areas.

Here are some general concepts and ideas pertaining to sharing the arts with your child that will make the experience rewarding and effective.

Until your child has learned enough to make her own decisions about her education in the arts, it will be up to you to introduce her to works she may appreciate. One way to go about this is to simply share with her the art that you love. What books or poems have captured your imagination over the years? Which movies make your all-time favorites list? Which lithographs could you stare at for hours? Tell her how you discovered these pieces and why you love them. Another approach is to use your knowledge of her own character and personality to cue you in on what may appeal to her. What is she naturally drawn to on television, in her hobbies, in her clothing choices? Pachelbel may be a great fit for the dreamy, contemplative child while Rachmaninoff may be your energetic child's new favorite composer. A comic book fan may find Lichtenstein's art worth the discovery and the empathetic child with a budding sense of social justice may fall right into step with Les Misérables.

There is also the chance that she may feel overwhelmed by your suggestions if you do not adopt a policy of inclusion from the very beginning. If you insist on only exposing your child to certain forms of artistic expression you both are guaranteed to miss out on countless, exemplary cultural experiences. If your child thinks vampire romances are the epitome of great literature she will not love them less because you insist it will be Charles Dickens or nothing. Your rigidity will only makes it more likely that she will be unwilling to consider other books you might choose for her. Likewise, if she loves the latest pop band, she will continue to, no matter how many times you tell her that the Beatles are much more worthy. A better approach is to share stories with her about the bands you loved at her age and the bands your parents loved at that same age. Then take the positive experience you have just created and turn it into a growth opportunity. Dust off some of your old records or go online with her and watch videos of bands she listens to. Then show her videos that take you down memory lane. When you were young and feeling completely over everyone and everything, what songs made you feel better? She may see that she is not so different from kids in other generations after all. Who knows? She may become the only child in her class who can pick Frank Sinatra or Jimi Hendrix out of a lineup!

Make the classics an organic starting point to the artistic journey you want to take with her. No matter her present interests, you will be able to introduce her to the masters who perfected the genre first. Say, for example, your child listens to rap music and you do not do not like it at all. You now have a perfect opportunity to learn something about music that could take your opinions in a whole new direction. Discover who originated the form and what the cultural landscape was like at the time. Partner with your child as you discover this information. You may still end up hating rap music; or you may be surprised to learn that groups like Sugar Hill Gang and Run DMC used rhyming couplets and percussion to spread positive messages to urban youth.

Regardless, you are demonstrating something very important to your child - when we are exposed to new things we are embracing growth and expanding our horizons. Few things engender sophistication as effectively as this realization. It also places your interests and your child's on a continuum where both extremes gain credibility and everything in between becomes something interesting and exciting to discover together. She might be intrigued to discover what influenced Handel's Messiah and you might likewise be fascinated by underground coalitions of spray paint taggers who may be changing the face of urban reactionary art. Besides, at some point even Brontë, Picasso and De Niro were considered upstarts. Let her know that there is room for her choices and personality. She will continue to see you as an ally and your suggestions will hit home nearly every time. Remaining curious, open-minded and patient will set a good example for your child and increases the odds that she, too, will be a lifelong learner.

Ask your child provocative questions about the arts and when doing so don't be afraid to use appropriate terms and expressions. She cannot identify or understand motifs, allegories, crescendos, film noire or bunraku forms if you shy away from using the terms. Help her filter her experiences by asking her what a piece reminded her of or how it made her feel.

Find ways to make art relevant by connecting its significance to everyday life. There will be countless opportunities to associate a book, song, painting, play, or dance to something that is going on around us. The can even be done with younger children. For example, you can prompt your younger child to discover the shapes in everyday objects. This will prepare her to identify form and structure in sculptures, murals and sketches. If your older child has a rocky day at school, teasingly ask her if it was Catcher in the Rye bad or Lord of the Flies bad? When she doesn't understand the connection she will be curious to know more. When she does understand it she will feel quite proud of herself for being astute. Either outcome is a win-win!

When planning excursions to theaters, museums, concert venues and galleries make every effort to learn as much about the space as possible before you go. Knowing exactly where the Reformation paintings are located, for example, will prevent you from losing the time you have allocated for that purpose. This will also help you establish a content-rich narrative that you can share with your child, building anticipation for the trip. Guarantee her comfort by making sure she is dressed for the weather and wears comfortable walking shoes. She will also get more out of the day if she is fed and rested and if the duration of the excursion is appropriate for her age and attention span.

Take advantage of the family membership packages many venues offer. The discounted rates encourage multiple visits, giving you even more reasons to take your time and allow your child to get maximum benefit from each trip. Memberships also come loaded with enticing extras such as early admissions, notifications of coming events, gift shop discounts, pre-sale ticket availability, summer exploration camps and workshops, private viewings and the ability to bypass long admission lines.

When selecting events to attend with your child, we recommend that you think outside the box for originality and experimentation. The community theater in your city or town may be renowned for its productions but a student performance piece at a nearby college or university can be just as praiseworthy and enjoyable. Perhaps a local bookstore owner turns his establishment over to sculptors once a month or the dance studio across town has a merengue mixer every other weekend. The farmer's market you frequent may sponsor a bluegrass festival in the spring with free pottery glazing lessons for beginners. Many publications and websites keep readers abreast of the latest art and entertainment news and can be a valuable source for both classic and unorthodox cultural possibilities.

Below are several suggestions, arranged by category, for projects and activities designed to give you and your child an amazing, immersive experience as you explore the arts together.

The Fine Arts

Select a theme or motif with your child and discover as much of its artistic incarnations as possible together. For example, if your child is currently into dance this is a perfect time to introduce her to Degas, Fred Astaire, Alvin Ailey, Rodgers and Hammerstein and Bollywood, just to name an eclectic few.

If your child liked to paint or draw herself, ask her if you can commission a piece of original art for an upcoming dinner party or other family celebration. Tell her the nature of the event, give her a timeframe and then leave the conceptualization, medium and execution up to her. Your friends and family will be thrilled with the results and your child will have a start-to-finish understanding of the concept of artistic patronage.

Have your child take her favorite book or song and recreate the piece visually using art supplies. Ask her about her choice of medium? Does the piece mirror the theme of the writing or make artistic departures? Is it constricting or liberating to tell a story without words?

Play musical easels with your family. Arrange easels with canvas and paint supplies in a circle - the number of easels should equal the number of participants. Pick someone who will not be painting and put him in charge of the music. Next, decide what you are going to use as the subject and place it in the center of the room. An easel is removed. Each person will then paint the object until someone stops the music. Remove one easel. Then everyone circles the easels until the music starts again and races to get an available easel. This continues until only one easel is left and the winner is announced. Lastly, arrange the incomplete art in order of elimination and encourage everyone to notice the progression of the piece as well as how several different people will see and recreate completely different components of the same object.

Encourage your child to turn her original art into gift worthy items such as calendars, note cards, canvas tote bags, t-shirts etc. Her dad will be proud to hang a calendar featuring her black and white photography on his wall at work. If she prefers three-dimensional art, have her take a photograph of the finished project in order to accomplish the same goal.

Help your child craft derivative art from her favorite needlework, weaving, bead working or jewelry piece. Her stained glass version of a panel from the Bayeux tapestry is sure to be a beautiful, one-of-a-kind conversation starter.

Literature

Start a family book club. After completing a book together have a party to celebrate, with the theme of the book providing the inspiration for the food, decorations and games.

Introduce your child to the joy of collecting by helping her purchase vintage books. You can start by sharing books with her that were a staple of your own childhood or even those of your parents. Read them with her and then go on the hunt for early editions of the books. The fun of scouring secondhand bookstores and consignment shops together will be matched only by the thrill of discovering a first edition copy of a book you have both come to love.

Craft a book cover wall with your child. Photocopy the covers of your favorite books, making sure they are not much bigger than the size of a postcard, and frame them. Hang them on the wall and explain to her that once a month you will both add a new book cover to the collection. She will be excited to see her collection growing along with your own and if the books are ones you have enjoyed together the experience will be that much more rewarding.

Listen to audiobooks with your child, especially during drive time or on weekends when there is more time. Afterwards watch any screen adaptations of the book and compare notes. Which version is better and why? If you had seen the movie before having read the book would you have gotten the same meaning from it? What may have prompted the changes from book to screen? Who would you have cast to play the book's characters and why?

Similar to our game of musical easels help your child host a writing swap party with several of her friends. Using notebooks or blank journals, each child begins a story or poem. When a five minute timer goes off each guest passes her book to the person on her left and they resume the story for the next five minutes. After half an hour or so the guests can read aloud the stories they each began.

The Performing Arts

Ask your child to create a music playlist for a party, family game night or any other organized gathering. This will get her to think of music in different ways. Should music accompany a theme or does music create the theme? How does music influence the tone and mood of a gathering? Is there a noticeable shift in energy among the guests when the energy of the music changes? What does this say about the power of music to help people emote?

Who is her favorite musician? Start a long-term exploration of his or her work with your child. Include music, videos, biographies, print articles and documentaries in your research. How did the artist change over the years both personally and artistically? Can these changes be traced to any significant events in his life or career? What music influenced the artist during his formative years? Are those influences evident in his early recordings and, if so, when did the artist's current style solidify? In what ways can music become a person's story?

Create musical tributes to friends and family members. If a favorite teacher is retiring your child can make a CD with songs that represent her regard for him, were popular the year he was born or became her teacher, reflect the subject matter he taught, etc. Your child can then have all of her classmates sign the CD jacket and present it to the teacher on his last day.

Sign your child up for music lessons. There is an instrument for everyone; try several, if necessary, until you find the right one. Few children are destined to become virtuosos but the benefit of music lessons is the technical immersion into the discipline and enjoyment of learning and performing. Despite the level of mastery achieved, few adults regret having taken music lessons as children. And for those who are still proficient on their instrument, the sense of accomplishment, the admiration of listeners, and the enhanced appreciation of music as a whole surely made the hours of lessons well worth it.

Give certain family occasions a specific soundtrack. For example, play Yo-Yo Ma in the background for Wednesday pasta night or the Motown Christmas album on repeat each year while you trim the tree. This continuity will give your child an appreciation of musical tradition. Years into adulthood she may still play Simon and Garfunkel's greatest hits when she takes her own family on a summer road trip!

Make some popcorn and have everyone take turns playing songs from their own playlists. This is a fun opportunity to learn new music and spark some great conversations. If you listen closely you will see what people are trying to tell you about themselves by the music they choose to share with others.

Before heading to the opera with your child spend a little time reading a translation of the piece. If possible, view it beforehand on film or online. This helps her focus on the skill and beauty of the dramatization instead of struggling to make sense of the scenes.

Spend an evening watching television with your child, allowing her to choose the programs. Afterward have a casual conversation with her about what you've seen. Does she prefer shows that seem realistic and plausible or does she watch them as a form of escapism? Do the shows have a diverse cast of characters? Are these characters depicted favorably or are they supporting characters for the show's leads? What kinds of companies advertise for certain types of shows? Do the lifestyles depicted in the programs match the products being advertised? What does this say about consumerism and art?

Help her organize a mini film festival with her friends. After selecting a theme – for example, movies with strong female characters -- let your child select three or four movies that meet the theme's criteria. On the day of the judging she can invite her friends over and make it an all-day event. An explanation of why she selected her theme and the criteria that each film selected would make an excellent round table discussion for her and her friends. Afterwards she can give them ballots and instruct them on the voting procedures. After a fun day of movies and snacks the group can vote on the films, choose a winner and continue the discussion throughout the rest of your child's mini film festival. For younger children costumes based around the movie theme can be especially entertaining.

Purchase children's movies and DVDs for your child in foreign languages. The simplistic themes and language make them easier for her to understand and enjoy. This also works surprisingly well for teenagers. A young adult soap opera follows a typical story arc, even if it is in Korean. A dating disaster is a dating disaster in any language!

Commission an homage video from your budding director or producer. Say, for example, that her Aunt Rebecca has a birthday coming up and you are having everyone over for a celebratory dinner. Let your child record interviews with the special people in her aunt's life, letting them share birthday wishes or recount fond memories. Afterward, your child (with help if necessary) can edit the footage, add narration, music, and credits, and compile it into a video. The video can be shown at the end of the party and a copy given to the guest of honor. Supervise the project but try to let your child do as much of the work as possible.

Perhaps your child can try making a documentary. Is she expecting a new brother or sister? Is a friend in training, hoping for a spot on her school's competitive cheerleading squad? Chronicling the journey and the outcome of a much anticipated event can be an educational and rewarding experience for your child.

When watching a DVD or movie with her make sure not to skip the extra features or behind the scenes footage. This broadens her understanding of the art and business of filmmaking.

If your child is interested in acting, take her to an audition. Give her the requirements beforehand and help her if she is unsure which monologue or song to learn for the audition.

Encourage your child to use brief, video snippets of herself as virtual greeting cards for family members who live out of town or who otherwise do not see her often.

Hopefully, some of these suggestions will allow you to incorporate a meaningful appreciation of the arts into your child's life. The satisfaction and enlightenment she will gain as a result will broaden her horizons and factor into her personal growth for many delightful years to come.

Chapter 10
The Perfect Host

"Friendship, is unnecessary, like philosophy, like art... it has no survival value, rather it is one of those things that gives value to survival."
CS Lewis

Spending quality time with friends, family and acquaintances is one of our most life-affirming activities, especially when there is something momentous to celebrate. Children are never too young to participate in these festivities and after this chapter you will see ways in which your child can become a charming host in his own right.

As we are fond of saying, your example can be your child's best teacher. Whether it is a birthday party for 20 or an intimate dinner for 6 let him take part in every aspect of your party planning. The more you get your child involved, the more he will develop an organic understanding of the components of good hosting. Ask him which china might work best with the tablescape. Introduce him to your caterer or florist before you begin your consultation. Allow him to suggest menu items and share your thoughts about his choices. His exposure to these details over time will help him to become at ease with the process.

Life presents countless opportunities to celebrate; the sophisticated child need not focus solely on birthdays and holidays. If cousin Caleb is visiting from out of state your child can invite his friends over for a small mixer to welcome and introduce him. Caleb will feel honored at his cousin's regard for him and your child's friends will be pleased to have made a new acquaintance. Any extended stay or visit by family or friends is a wonderful reason to host an affair.

Other reasons include accomplishments both great and small. Qualifying for the swim team, making it through finals and being accepted into a competitive program are all examples of life events to celebrate together. With a little practice and experience your child will be able to host such parties with the best of them. Giving him guidance as he puts his learning into practice will inspire confidence and spark his creativity.

Planning

Once your child has identified an occasion for entertaining he must begin to plan. While a small notebook or blank journal is useful during the planning stages, your tech-savvy child may prefer keeping a file on his PC or tablet. Whatever medium he chooses, keeping track of his ideas as well as the guest list reduces the chance of making costly mistakes and budgeting errors. He should also keep a folder to help him keep up with receipts and vendor contracts. If the florist's invoice erroneously lists $25 worth of Gerber daisies and your child has the original contract he will be able to more easily resolve the situation.

Likewise, record keeping will help him stay within the budget. Whether he is entertaining from his own funds or with an allowance from you any spending should be done with care and common sense. If you are footing the bill give your child an operating budget designed to get the job done effectively but without allowing him to feel that money is no object, even should this be the case. Working within a predetermined budget makes him much more likely to pay attention to details, make more informed choices and use his creativity to get around any monetary obstacles to his vision.

Saving his notes may also prove useful for future reference. Your child may have forgotten that he served lemon chicken with pasta at his friend Naomi's pre-Bat Mitzvah bash and is planning to serve it again to almost the same guests.

The sooner he begins planning the better. This will allow him the time to deal with any issues that pop up and make the implementation of new ideas easier. Determining a theme is an important but fun part of entertaining. Even events with that come with their own themes can be tweaked to come up with a sub theme. For example, if your son has a get together to celebrate his soccer team's championship the theme would obviously be soccer. But giving the party an awards night theme could take the party in a different and exciting direction. Setting up a red carpet entrance, providing a podium and mic for 'acceptance speeches' and allowing guests to put together an interview montage to be viewed afterwards -- this is an example of a party theme that followed a different path.

The Guest List

Often, the nature of the occasion determines most of the guest list. However, You can also encourage your child to think outside of the box when it comes to who will be attending. Friends from different areas of his world may enjoy meeting one another. Perhaps Sadie, the super smart girl in his debate club would get along perfectly with A'Lexus, the outgoing star of her soccer team. Bringing interesting and dynamic people together is what the consummate host does best.

Steer your child away from engaging in social politics when composing his guest list. An invitation should not be used as a way to curry favor with people your child thinks are cool or can do something for him. Nor should invitations be based on looks, popularity or other superficialities. Teach your child that a caring friend with integrity is one whose character doesn't change based on the situation at hand. If two friends are at odds your child should refrain from taking sides or deciding which friend to invite and which friend to deny an invitation. He should simply invite them both, as a true friend would do. Showing preference will inevitably lead to hurt feelings. Perhaps both parties involved may come to an understanding based on the excellent judgement and fairness shown by your child.

Invitations

Attractive invitations with themes and characters are available in most stationery stores. Alternatively, you can encourage your child to design his own invitations or use simple, clean stock paper that can be embellished by hand or left as is for a truly sophisticated look. Regardless of whether he used pre-printed of homemade invitations, he should address them by hand if is it practical, and sign each invitation.

For smaller parties your child can consider adding special touches that will capture the tone of the event. For example, he can tuck the invitation to his beach party inside small plastic bottles, purchased online or at craft stores. An invitation to a graduation party could be designed to look like a diploma and shipped in a mailing tube. His imagination can be his guide.

For more formal parties, save the date cards or emails should be sent at least two months before the event. This gives the guests a chance to manage their schedules around the party and it gives your child a preliminary idea of who may or may not be attending. A proper invitation should follow and should be sent to guests no later than three weeks prior to the event.

As responses begin to arrive your child should make a note of who has accepted and who has declined. Remind him that it is impolite to ask an invitee why they have declined an invitation. Chances are high that they will volunteer the information themselves or your child will already know the reason. If that is not the case, however, your child should graciously refrain from putting anyone on the spot.

Food and Drink

Delightful food and drinks are most certainly the foundation of any great party. If your child has developed some cooking skills, this is a time when he can show them off. If he is not planning on cooking, he can still show off his skills in picking crowd pleasing foods. Whether snacks, heavy appetizers, a buffet, or a seated dinner, help your child select foods that fit the style and theme of the event.

For example, a baked potato bar at a pool party would not be the best idea for guests. Full cutlery is required, baked potatoes are not necessarily light, summer fare and it is not a food that is easy to stroll around a pool with. In this scenario a fajita station or a barbecue would be much more conducive to a great time. Your child will have a good idea of what his friends like and his menu planning skills will improve as you both observe what works and what does not.

Teach your child to have reasonable expectations regarding the food he plans to serve. In addition to budgetary concerns he must decide how much attention he wants to spend on preparation and serving during the course of the party. If he is throwing a going away party for a friend who will be studying abroad he will want to keep the menu easy and manageable - spending time with his friend and the other guests will take precedence over making sure the Thai curry puffs do not burn.

If the menu is too overwhelming or otherwise labor intensive he will be too preoccupied to be at his best with the guests. Mingling, seeing to everyone's comfort and spending time talking and laughing with everyone in attendance will make a lasting impression - people may or may not remember what they ate. To this end, let your child start small and work his way up. The food can be partially catered, partially pre-made or made in advance so that he can focus on the other aspects of entertaining.

If there are any guests with special dietary concerns your child should plan the menu so as not to exclude these people from enjoying the meal along with the other guests. They will find it commendable that he made this extra effort.

Regardless of the menu show your child how to serve everything in an attractive and inviting manner. For example, pale foods such as rice pilaf or hummus look tastier when served in vibrantly colored dishes and with a bit of parsley or fresh thyme sprinkled on top. Let your child be creative in serving beverages.

Putting iced bottles of sparkling water in a child's wagon, for instance, is a charming idea for a backyard bash.

Occasionally look through cooking and entertaining magazines for menu ideas with your child. Point out how prepared food items are displayed and presented in magazines, online, on packaging and on television. He will begin to spot recurring themes as he develops his own sense of what will be appealing and appetizing when serving guests.

Finishing Touches

Designing the look of the party will allow your child's originality and creativity to shine through. He will begin to develop his own talent for choosing the flowers, tablescapes and accents that will bring his gathering to life.

It goes without saying that music adds interest and enjoyment to gatherings and this is another area where your child will grow increasingly knowledgeable and intuitive. Help him choose music that is appropriate and reflects the general tone of the event. His favorite band may not be as appreciated at a party his grandparents are attending, for example. His playlist should attempt to reflect the tastes of the majority of his guests. This is not to say that he cannot expose others to music that is new for them. Different types of music may work well for different phases of the party.

Should your child have a friend or acquaintance who plays a musical instrument or sings your child might want to approach him during the planning stages and ask him to perform at the party. More than likely the person will feel honored that your child thinks highly of his talent and will be more than happy to further hone his craft live.

Other decisions, such as deciding on party favors, whether or not to have gift bags and what entertainment to have should have as much of your child's input as possible. This is how he will eventually grow into the role of host.

Excellent manners, as always, should be front and center. Your child should make himself available at the start and end of every gathering he hosts. Greeting each guest individually will make them feel welcome and ease them into the social flow of the party. Teach your child to be aware of the needs of his guests and make sure that everyone is enjoying himself. He should spend at least a few minutes with each guest at larger gatherings and introduce people who do not yet know each other when he can. As the party comes to a close your child should personally say goodbye to each guest and thank him or her for attending.

Hosting Ideas

Help your child plan an age appropriate television awards party. Whether it's the Kid's Choice Awards for your pop culture guru, the Grammy's for your music lover or the Oscars for your movie buff, awards programs are a great reason to gather friends for a viewing party. Before the show your child can have guests write their predictions down on pieces of paper which are then 'locked' away until all the awards have been announced. The guest with the most accurate guesses receives a prize.

Social consciousness begins with awareness and what better reason for your child to host an event? Encourage him to invite friends over in the name of a worthy cause. A relevant documentary can be the highlight of the evening and perhaps your child could solicit small donations in support of an associated charitable cause.

Your child can host an all-day tournament followed by dinner and recognitions. Tennis, croquet, chess, volleyball - the possibilities are endless.

A book themed party is an excellent way to bring people together and may even inspire your child and his friends to start a book club. Spirited discussion of the book along with a viewing of a related film or documentary can be as entertaining as it is enlightening.

Help your child plan a State of the Union or presidential debate viewing party. A presidential trivia contest might be a good ice breaker at the beginning of the evening. Guests can help your child decorate a U.S. flag cake with blueberries, strawberries and whipped cream and the guest with the birthday closest to the president's receives a small prize.

Whatever occasion brings your child's guests together, they will consider themselves fortunate to have a friend who is such a considerate, talented and sophisticated host.

Chapter 11
Wellness

"A good laugh and a long sleep are the best cures in a doctor's book."
Irish Proverb

Considerable attention has recently been given to the current state of child health in the US. According to recent studies the rate of obesity in children ages 6 to 11 has increased fivefold over the last 30 years and has tripled in adolescents. A two-pronged approach to combat this problem consists of improved nutrition and physical exercise to help children lead healthier lives. In this chapter we adopt a holistic approach to healthy eating and exercise as well as other aspects of your child's well-being such as managing stress, social support, and the components of a beneficial environment.

A holistic approach to wellness works best because quality medical care alone is not capable of addressing your child's needs. Behavior and environment play a much larger role in how we feel, think and function and no one has more control over these factors than do parents. Many of the topics covered in the other chapters of this book have a direct bearing on your child's wellness. The poise and confidence she gains over time will directly enhance her emotional well-being which, in turn, is intimately linked to her physical health.

An example can further illustrate the necessity of a holistic approach: A father limits his son's social activities because he fears any peer rejection may trigger a bout of anxiety, a condition for which his son is already receiving clinical counseling. This decision, however, keeps the child indoors for the majority of the time he is not at school. Out of boredom and a growing realization that he is not connecting with his peers the child plays video games, posts in online gaming forums and snacks on microwave pizza bites, chips and sodas. His poor eating habits and sedentary lifestyle lead to eventual weight gain which in turn makes him feel tired, lethargic and self-conscious. In turn, his father becomes even more protective of his increasingly unhappy child. The negative feedback loop continues.

On the other hand, we can also imagine an anxiety prone child who is very active in athletics. Sports keep him fit and within his recommended weight range and it promotes better sleep. These things result in improved mood and energy and fewer anxiety attacks. Less boredom and stress also make compulsive eating less likely. His emotional well-being is enhanced both by physical fitness and by his relationships with his teammates. His father, now not as worried about his son's anxiety, feels free to encourage him in a variety of other areas. The positive feedback loop continues.

It is clear from these opposing examples that good health is not simply a matter of dealing with illnesses as they arise. The components of a fit and healthy life cannot be considered one at a time – they are inextricably bound together.

Nutrition

As you can discern from our chapter on "The Cultivated Palate" we are not ones to recommend austerity when it comes to great food! But it is not fine dining that has led to America's obesity problem. Mostly processed foods, starchy and high in fat, as well as overly-large portion sizes have caused this epidemic. The good news is that because habits form early you can instill different nutritional priorities in your child if you start when she is young.

From the time your child is small, make a distinction between healthy and unhealthy foods and beverages. As she gets older, talk to her about why certain foods are better for her than others. If your daughter drinks milk, for example, she should know that milk contains calcium and vitamin D and know that these nutrients are important because of the role they play in developing strong bones and teeth. She should know why drinking water is important and the best choice when she feels thirsty. Read food labels with her so she can begin to understand exactly what she is consuming. She will make her own food choices when she gets older, but she is much more likely to construct a healthy diet for herself if she has been educated about nutrition.

Exercise and Fitness

While good nutrition is crucial to a holistic approach to health and wellness, it is only one aspect. Regular exercise is important not only for the direct benefit it has on physical well-being, but also for its positive psychological and emotional effects.

Almost everyone is aware that exercise is crucial for cardiovascular health and the prevention of obesity and Type 2 diabetes. It also increases blood flow which aids cells with oxygen absorption. More oxygen absorption means greater energy for your child to engage in all of the activities and new experiences that we talk about in this book.

Exercise also enhances brain metabolism, which improves concentration, reduces anxiety , elevates mood and can catalyze the intellectual development you want for your child.

Another benefit of exercise is that it enhances self-esteem and confidence. Some of this results from the sense of strength and physical integrity that fitness provides. Some of it comes from mastering a specific skill; for example, learning to ride a bicycle or being able to hold a difficult position in yoga. This sense of mastery does not require involvement in a competitive sport. It comes from personal, internal challenges.

That said, children can benefit tremendously from competitive sport. The mental constancy that comes from goal-focused skill development carries over into school and career goals. For these reasons college admissions officers and prospective employers are often impressed with extensive levels of involvement in an organized sport.

In addition to these positive aspects of involvement in sport, there are the benefits that come from being associated with a team. It is undoubtedly possible to get the benefits of teamwork in other arenas. Competitive sports, however, provide a ready-made situation in which a group of kids will be pulling together towards a particular goal. Adults whose competitive days are far behind them often report that their relationships with teammates are among the closest they have ever formed.

This closeness seems to occur regardless of the sport being played. Both team and individual sports such as football, basketball, wrestling, gymnastics, track and field etc require a good deal of what's known as task cohesion. This inevitably leads to the development of social cohesion; teammates with a shared goal come to care about each other.

So regardless of the sport the social and physical benefits for your child can be enormous. Unfortunately, it is also possible for sports to be a place for the development of anxiety and the promotion of unsavory behavior. It is important, then, to make it clear that wins or losses are not why you are proud of her athletic endeavors. If she is enjoying her sport -- and especially if she is putting forth her best effort -- it is very likely that she is getting out of sports what she needs. If she is not enjoying it, she should feel free to explore other avenues for fitness and fun. Some children do not enjoy activities where direct competition with others is the vehicle for success. These children may be better suited to sports that challenge individuals to succeed by doing their personal best, such as archery, skiing and figure skating. Whenever possible use your child's personality and interests to help her find the physical activity that is right for her. Does she love animals and have a sense of elegance and showmanship? Dressage may be a good fit for her. Is she in love with ancient mythology or movies with strong, adventurous female leads? Ask her if she might like archery or fencing lessons. There is a sport or enjoyable physical activity for every child.

If you begin to notice that your child's emotional investment is leading to inappropriate behavior she must be reminded of the importance of good conduct and true sportsmanship. Few things are more unsavory to observe than seeing an athlete have a tantrum or blame others for her team's misfortune. Good manners and best practices certainly do not go out of the window simply because we are engaged in competition.

The Social and Physical Environment

Nutrition and exercise are important but they must be accompanied by a healthy environment -- one free from unmanageable stressors with positive and supportive social relationships. Careful attention to the health behaviors we have already discussed are only likely to result in good health if they take place in an environment with these characteristics.

Structure, routine and organization gives your child a sense of coherence and security. This will allow her the freedom to explore and push boundaries. School aged children must have a clean, quiet, environment for their studies. A dedicated spot for doing homework (e.g. a bedroom desk) is a must for academic success.

You should not completely shield your child from stress and responsibility. Stress is inescapable in the lives of most adults so you cannot achieve your goal of raising an accomplished individual unless you allow her to experience (and learn to cope with) adversity. On the other hand, overwhelming levels of stress only serve to teach a child that her coping efforts are inevitably ineffective. If your child seems down or is displaying anxiety, consider whether the circumstances of her environment have changed or if her routine has been disrupted.

The more resources your child has for coping with stressful circumstances the more likely she is to avoid feeling distressed and may even gain confidence and competence from the successful resolution of the situation. Research has demonstrated that perhaps the most important resource is social support. Children of good parents usually feel loved but it is equally important that they feel valued and esteemed. Interestingly, children do not automatically come by these important traits just because their parents love them unconditionally - children must be made to feel they have worth. Sometimes the things we earn give us more validation than the things we are given. Studies have shown that people feel better about themselves and their accomplishments when they are unaware that someone was actually helping them to accomplish it. When the help being received is obvious it can convey a sense of weakness or incompetence to the recipient.

It important to impart this information to your child in order to help her put her own compassion and empathy into proper perspective. To be a good friend and to help others when and where she can, it is important to not call attention to the effort. Your child will learn the satisfaction of helping others without needing the credit that can potentially come with it.

Mental Health

A relatively ordered and supportive environment, together with consistent physical health, will go a long way towards promoting psychological well-being in your child. Symptoms of psychological distress, anxiety in particular, are nonetheless common in pre-teen and teenage children. They usually result from the stressors that are part and parcel of growing up and coming of age. Also, as your child enters into adolescence her social interactions begin to contain some adult elements and adult feelings. Unfortunately, this happens without the benefit of the actual experience that most adults enjoy. The activities and experiences we have suggested in this book will provide a valuable and useful layer of preparation for this difficult life stage.

Nonetheless, it is unlikely that your child will entirely escape occasional periods of adolescent angst, depressed mood or general anxiety. Most of these issues will be at a sub-clinical level. This means that they involve manageable levels of distress that are entirely normal for your child's life stage. This does not mean that these feelings are inconsequential. Let your child know that you have sympathy for what she is going through and respect for how she is handling it. Do not change how you treat your child; you should still engage her in challenging ways and still have age-appropriate expectations of her.

It is important to be available to talk about feelings and problems; as often as you can allow such discussions to be on your child's terms. If your see that she seems overwrought, get her to help you with a household chore; tasks requiring moderate levels of focus are often best for taking the edge off of anxious feelings. Is she nervous because her best friend didn't call her at the agreed upon time? Ask her to help you sort your recipe cards by category. The current popularity of adult coloring books is a testament to the calming effect of detail oriented preoccupation. Play music in the background and gradually start a conversation about what is causing her distress. She may prefer not to talk about it at that time, but knowing that you were willing to listen has benefits of its own.

If yours is a religious family, encourage your child to be open to the tenets of her faith. Even in the absence of religion, a sense of spirituality can help her through tough times. Many types of exercise, such as yoga or tai chi, have a spiritual dimension thereby providing her with physical fitness and spiritual nourishment at the same time. You can create opportunities for her to meditate. Even if you do not call it meditation, your child should have a personal space for some mindful quiet time; space that is respected by the rest of the family. Encourage your child to make taking this kind of time a lifelong habit, particularly during stressful periods.

It is not uncommon for mood and anxiety problems to reach a level at which your child may benefit from professional intervention. If this becomes necessary it should be done seamlessly, just as you might take her to the doctor if her sore throat persisted for too long, unrelieved by your honey lemon tea. Your relationship with her will remain unchanged as she enters treatment and so you must be firm in your insistence that other individuals in her life follow the same behavior. This will counteract the stigma and negative stereotypes surrounding mental health problems that your child may have observed in the media or through her social interactions.

The Pubescent Child

A potential source of anxiety as your child enters her pre-teen and teen years will be her entrance into puberty. The physical changes involved are profound and your teen will also have to deal with new feelings associated with the hormonal changes involved. For girls, puberty is the point at which the risk for depression becomes considerably elevated; twice that for boys of similar age. Much of this risk may be related to hormones and the fact that girls mature at a slightly faster rate than do boys of the same age. And children are observant. Your child may compare her pubescent development to those of her peers, just as they will to hers. The resulting emotions can include awkwardness, embarrassment, self-consciousness and low self-esteem.

You should begin to talk about puberty with your child long before it actually occurs. Part of the distress that comes with this life stage is a result of the confusion it engenders. If your child is prepared for the experience, she will be better able to cope with the changes involved. Somewhat later, you can begin to talk with her about the social changes she can expect as both she and her friends and classmates go through puberty. With planning and information she can enter this stage of development with the confidence that comes from knowledge and preparation. Another benefit to talking about puberty with your child is that you will be sure that she is getting accurate information and sound advice from you and not her peers.

The onset of puberty also necessitates talking with your child about sex. You may have already begun this conversation with her and feel satisfied that only supplemental information is needed. Or perhaps this is an entirely new area of health and wellness that you and your child have had no need to address before. In either case the same principles apply with regards to sex education as they do to topics such as grooming, good manners, interpersonal communications, etc. Take the lead in establishing a safe space for discourse and give your child the freedom and security to ask questions and express her thoughts and opinions.

These are not always comfortable or easy conversations to have but a truly sophisticated child is one who has been given the appropriate tools to manage complicated subject matter and process new information with clarity and poise. Your example is the best instructor. No two families are alike in how they educate their children about sexuality and sexual health. A wide array of factors such as value systems, religious beliefs and personal preferences will guide the timing, tone and content of your discussion with your child. In addition, young adults vary dramatically in their maturity levels and readiness for the potential emotional implications of becoming sexually active.

Encouragingly, research has been quite uniform in demonstrating that learning about contraception and safe-sex practices does not increase an adolescent's likelihood of becoming sexually active. Your child needs to be knowledgeable about these practices well before she needs them herself. It is equally important that she becomes aware of the potential emotional implications of considering or engaging in sex. This knowledge becomes especially valuable because, despite her personal level of interest in sex, she will be a part of a peer group for whom the topic will form a substantial part of their daily dialogue. She will benefit from warnings about confusing sexual activity and intimacy. If you can imagine your child armed with self-confidence and the knowledge about sex she has gained from your input, then you will feel much more confident about her ability to navigate these waters safely and happily.

Information on the topic of promoting wellness in the developing child could fill an entire book on its own. It is our hope that this chapter has made clear the important part played by physical and emotional wellness in your child's development. A holistic approach to managing your child's wellness plan ensures she will have the best opportunities possible to grow into a happy and healthy adult.

Suggestions and Ideas

Introduce your child to sparkling water and seltzer. Most children love the fizzy stuff but soda has no nutritional value and is frighteningly high in sugar. Even sugar free versions of popular carbonated beverages contain chemical sweeteners that do not add any value to your child's diet. Club soda can give your child an alternative to sodas - reserve it for special occasions when a splash of grenadine or sweetened lime juice can make it feel festive. If she has already developed a taste for soda, introduce her to seltzer or club soda that has been diluted with lemon-lime soda, gradually reducing the amount of soda over time. For toddlers, juice should be diluted with water by half although fresh fruit is by far the best choice.

Create a meditation or "chill out" space with your child. Encourage her to determine which colors, themes, sights and sounds she responds to and use this information to create a one of a kind space for her to use when she needs to escape. Does she love the beach? Place a cozy ottoman near a window with a great view add soft, overstuffed pillows. A small occasional table with a glass bowl of sand and seashells, an ocean breeze scented candle and a great novel may be the retreat she needs to recharge her batteries after a long day.

In good weather months take your child to the park to participate in yoga or tai chi. Skill or proficiency will be relatively minor issues as you both embrace a natural, low-impact approach to wellness.

Designate a day of the week to take brisk sunset walks or bike rides with your family. Take along a few ripe, juicy apples or pears but leave the portable music and earbuds at home! You will be pleasantly surprised at how much conversation your children are eager to participate in when they have no other distractions.

Host a day of Olympic-style games in your backyard. Put your child in charge of planning the games, judging criteria, healthy snacks and prizes for the day. Encourage her to invite her friends to spend the day racing, running and jumping their way into wellness.

Find or purchase a zany, festive hat and designate it the family feedback hat. Whomever is wearing the hat gets to spend the entire day receiving compliments, hugs and other forms of positive, interpersonal feedback. The key to success is to actively focus on the person's positive achievements slightly more than how much you love and adore him.

Spend the day at a local farm or orchard with your child. Many offer scheduled, seasonal activities for families and welcome visitors to gift shops and restaurants on the premises. Your child will have a greater respect for where her food comes from and the tasty benefits of eating fresh, locally sourced foods.

Give your child access to healthy snacks, especially during times when she may be feeling stressed or tired, as these are times when people are more likely to make poor choices. Nuts, berries, fresh fruit, trail mix, baked tortilla chips and salsa and dill pickle spears are examples of snacks you can feel good about giving to your child.

Whenever possible try to run errands with your child just after breakfast or lunch. This increases the likelihood that you will be home before it's time for the next meal - decreasing the likelihood that you will grab fast food to tide you over because you're famished.

Create a brag board for your child filled with photos, ribbons, notes and other mementos of their goals and achievements. This will reinforce her self-esteem and remind her that she is not only well loved, but is accomplished and capable in her own right.

Chapter 12

The Internet and Social Media

"Whether via social media or in person, building your relationships is a long-term process and the ultimate goal is to strengthen your network one person at a time.'
Raymond Arroyo

In these times no book dealing with parenting or manners and etiquette would be complete without an extended discussion about the internet and social media. Just about any piece of information available in the world can be accessed in moments via the internet.

Furthermore, the internet has become so user-friendly that, yes, even a child can do it. Indeed, having never known a world without the internet, modern teens and children are often more skilled at accessing what the web has to offer than are their parents. But while the internet is an invaluable resource for the developing sophisticate, it also has the potential for danger. Until your child is old enough and has acquired the social savvy you are trying to instill, it will be very important to steer her use of the internet in appropriate directions.

Unfortunately, nearly every benefit of the internet has a negative side for your child. On the one hand, it gives her the ability to research all manner of topics, instantly giving her the same amount of information that would have taken days in the library to access 25 years ago. Most schools already have students make extensive use of the internet in homework assignments. On the other hand, this easy access also makes information available that is entirely inappropriate for children to consume. Thus, for young children, use of the internet is best when it is strictly monitored.

We suggest that you make clear to your child the type of information you do not want her to access and, importantly, explain your reasons for the restriction. In this way, as her internet sophistication increases, so will her discernment as to the types of websites to avoid.

Another benefit of the web is the ease with which information can be shared with others: pieces of research can be shared with classmates for a joint assignment, pictures of a performance in the school play can be shared with grandparents. Here too, however, there are pitfalls. Your child should never share her name, address, telephone number, or the name of her school without your permission. Younger children should be clear that registering on on any website, even one that seems to be for children, also requires your permission. If you allow her to make a purchase online, you should examine the website beforehand to ensure it is legitimate. A sophisticated consumer knows the truth of the phrase caveat emptor - buyer beware - and it is particularly important with respect to internet purchases since there is often no accessible avenue for redress when something goes wrong.

Of course, we are all aware that one of the main uses people make of the internet is to share their ideas and opinions. This can usually be done anonymously which is good from the point of view of your child's safety as we have noted. However, it only takes a quick read through the comments section of any online news story to realize that anonymity has its downside. Hatred, intolerance and rampant cultural division are also entrenched parts of the social conversation.

We anticipate that most parents will feel that exposure to this component of the internet would not be in the best interests of their young child. At the same time, the educational benefits of the internet can allow parents to expose their children to the kind of history that can contextualize this hostility for her and prepare her to meet it later in her development, as she inevitably will.

These problems aside, the internet is truly a godsend for the parent wanting to raise an erudite child. With some structure in the ways that she engages this resource, it can provide a real jump-start to the goals you have for her. What follows are just a few suggestions on how to exploit the internet to further the development of your sophisticated child.

Help her to design and maintain a family website or blog. This can be updated with anecdotes from and about her family along with pictures, videos and sound clips. Help her locate guides and resources to make the site attractive and interesting. Out of town family and acquaintances will be especially appreciative of the project.

Start an online genealogy project with your child. Researching and documenting family history will quickly lead to an exploration of topics in history and culture. Just as importantly, the exercise will give you golden opportunities to share stories and memories from your own past.

Choose an age appropriate current event and locate online stories from both a conservative and a liberal news source. Have your child read the stories aloud and follow this with a discussion about differences in tone and content. Which facts did each publication choose to highlight? Did the tone of the viewer comments concur or conflict with those of the pieces? Ask your child which feature she liked better and why. Have a discussion about the nature and reliability of different sources when searching for information on the internet.

Social Media

For all of the educational potential of the internet, it is the social media component of the web that will attract increasing amounts of attention from your child as she gets older. As her friends obtain Facebook and Instagram accounts, the pressure will mount for her to have her own social media presence. Each parent must decide the age at which a child is ready for this exposure, but it will be important nonetheless to monitor your child's interactions until it is clear that her level of maturity justifies greater independence.

There are two characteristics children have in varying amounts that can cause problems on social media. The first is impulsiveness. Convey to your child that, once her posts are seen, they cannot be taken back. A thoughtlessly posted message can put her in a negative light, and often has the potential to hurt others. As she develops advanced communication skills in general, she is also likely to become more considerate about how she expresses herself through social media. The "pause and think" before you post is a good rule to follow, and you have to enforce that rule with her until you feel that she can enforce it independently.

The other characteristic that can be dangerous in the social media context is secretiveness. It is a rare child indeed, who goes through her preteen and teen years having an entirely open and honest relationship with her parents. The tension between the developing adult's increasing need for privacy and her parents' need to have the information necessary to act in her best interests, is one that gets negotiated in nearly every home.

The ubiquity of social media, however, puts these negotiations in an entirely different context. For one thing, the scope of the internet means that your child can end up in contact with individuals who do not share your values or who do not have her best interests at heart; indeed some may even seek to harm your child. In addition, communications on social media are, by definition, public to varying degrees. Thus, regardless of the degree of privacy you extend to your teenager, you should have access to what they are saying or displaying online.

There is no reason for your child to exclude you as a Facebook "friend" and you should not allow such secretiveness. Many problems can be avoided if your child accepts the fact that anything they would not say or do in front of you should certainly never appear on social media.

As the use of social media by teens and pre-teens has become commonplace so has the phenomenon of cyberbullying. It should be clear to your child that bullying of any kind would be a complete breach of the ethical and behavioral agreements between the two of you. If the lessons in this book have worked for you and your child is a confident, caring person with the skills to make others feel at ease in social situations, then this should carry over 100% to her social media presence.

Just as you would expect her to have a level of grace and sophistication that would preclude her participating in any cyberbullying, you would hope that her confidence and charisma would prevent her from becoming a victim, as well. Unfortunately, it does not always work this way. Indeed, your child may be put under attack precisely because of her sophistication and popularity.

This is another reason it is important to be personally connected to her social media. Kids who are victims of bullying experience high rates of depression, anxiety, disruptive behaviors, truancy and academic downturns. Make it clear to your child that you are an ally and a resource should she feel she is being bullied. Explicitly intervene with the school and with other parents if it becomes necessary. In many states parents can be held responsible, by law, for any actions that constitute cyberbullying by children living in the home.

The sophisticated child can and should also be an advocate for her peers. Encourage her to intervene on behalf of classmates who are being bullied. Such intervention may put her at odds with the perpetrators. At the same time, however, she is likely to become admired as a result of her advocacy. Support your child in these efforts. Locate your state's statutes on cyberbullying and study them carefully. Use age appropriate language and examples to share this information with your child. In this way you are sending her the message that you will always advocate for her and that, as a result, she has a safe space from which to advocate for others.

Teens and families have begun to be aware of an additional danger from social media. Private schools, colleges and universities, scholarship committees, internship directors, employers and even future romantic partners are increasingly relying on social media imprints to give them insight into a person's background and character. This has the potential of putting your child in the difficult position of having to explain her actions and decisions from several years prior. Stories abound of teens failing to be admitted to the college of their choice because of a bad decision recorded for posterity on the internet. Thus, you are well-advised to continually impress upon your child that the details of her life that she shares online never truly go away.

You may feel confident that your older teen has developed a level of sophistication that would preclude her embarrassing herself online. This could be entirely true and yet she could still be severely compromised by a friend with a cell phone who chooses to record a social event at an inopportune time; she may not even be aware that she is being recorded. Once again, if is something that she would not say or do in front of you, it is something that she might best not do at all.

In spite of all the potential pitfalls, the possibilities for entertainment, inspiration, and education offered by the internet make it an invaluable resource for the parent seeking to raise a sophisticated child. It can provide an unlimited number of journeys for the two of you to embark upon. It reinforces the aspects of her life that are positive and connects her to the world you are working hard to prepare her to successfully navigate.

Chapter 13
Conflict Management

"Where there is no struggle there is no strength."
Oprah Winfrey

Your child will have bad days. Giving him the tools he needs to navigate these days will benefit him throughout his lifetime. He will become resilient and will be less likely to let his anger, disappointment or frustration get the better of him and cause him to lose his poise and sense of decorum.

During his formative years the majority of your child's conflicts will involve you. As an authority figure and the mainstay in his limited world you are the one he will push back against, challenge and the one whose boundaries and resolve will be tested. As he grows the realm for potential conflict will expand to include peers, siblings and others with whom he has regular contact. The conflict management practices you teach him early on will help him deal with conflict when he encounters it out in the world.

As his parent your child is observing not only how you interact with him when problems arise but how you manage complex issues with others as well. Your behavior and approach will become the model for his behavior and inform his choices in future conflict situations.

Conflict can sometimes have positive outcomes. If your child is not allowed to have a difference of opinion with you or to protest things that he thinks are unfair or that are barriers to what he wants to do, his frustration is likely to come out in less constructive ways. The key is to teach him healthy, result-oriented ways in which to engage in a conflict; ways that get the points across while respecting the opinions and feelings of other people. With patience and positive feedback this will become easier for him over time. You will be proud that he has gained a level of integrity and self-control beyond that of many adults.

Often, our inclination as parents is to respond to poor behavior with punishment. However, there are more effective ways to teach your child to take responsibility for his actions. We suggest an approach that emphasizes with your child the consequences of his actions. For example if he has consistently failed to complete his algebra assignments it may seem reasonable to tell him he is going to be grounded. But this approach alone only sends the message that he has done something to make you unhappy so you are rectifying the situation by doing something to make him unhappy. What a chain reaction! It creates an opportunity for him to be distracted by the unpleasant dynamic that now exists between the two of you instead of dealing with the real issue - why he isn't doing his homework. It also gives him too much responsibility for your feelings and emotions and ties your approval of him to his performance as opposed to who he is as a person.

Alternatively, explain to him that failing to do his homework will result in poor grades. Therefore, as a parent, you will attempt to modify his behavior by restricting his privileges. In this way his poor academic performance becomes the 'punishment', if you will, and is seen as natural consequence of his choices. His loss of privileges becomes a remedy, your parental response to those consequences. The child thus retains his agency and can more clearly see the results of his choices even if he is not ready to change or improve. Furthermore, he is not struggling beneath the emotional weight of your reactions. He sees that you are governing your emotions and he will eventually use that as a model for his own reactions. In the long run, he will develop a mature approach to conflict -- one that is centered more around the problematic circumstances and events, and less on potentially misguided or inflated emotions.

When your child has negative interactions with his peers or siblings encourage him to find thoughtful and appropriate solutions. Emphasize the importance of discussing the problem without engaging in insults, raising one's voice, or otherwise creating an unpleasant scene. Nothing is less sophisticated than losing one's temper in public and being rude or insulting. Sometimes the more astute person simply has to walk away; few conflicts are worth a loss of dignity and fewer still are worth inciting serious strife or discord. Teach your child that it is better to table a discussion or disagreement until all parties are calm.

You cannot emphasize enough to your child the importance of listening carefully when someone is explaining why they are upset. Active listening means he is concentrating on what others are saying in order to absorb their full meaning as opposed to listening but mentally forming his response or rebuttal. After listening he should then paraphrase and give back what he just heard and follow this with a simple 'did I understand you properly?' Or 'is this what you meant?'. This the person respect and indicates a clear desire to truly understand the person is trying to convey. Often a conflict can be scaled down simply by listening to the person who is upset and giving validation to his or her concerns. The rest is just working out the details.

There will be times, however, when conflict is ongoing and no easy solutions are readily available or accessible. Teach your child that not all problems are solved overnight but patience and a willingness to communicate go a long way towards resolving almost any issue. Your first lessons in this regard will come from how you, yourself, interact with him when child-parent conflict occurs. Continue to treat him with respect and continuity even when the situation becomes protracted. For example, if he continues not to take his algebra seriously and you restrict his privileges, make every effort also to encourage and support him. The measures you take are designed to give him the space he needs to measure the weight of his decisions and their consequences. They do not need to be supplemented with criticism, or constant reminders of his shortcomings. Again, he will use your behavior to construct his own approach to conflict. So later, when he is frustrated because he feels his biology lab partner isn't pulling his weight on an important project, the situation will have a better chance of being favorably resolved because of the lessons he learned from you.

Conflict with others is inevitable for your child. While challenging, it is also an opportunity to for him to learn resilience and grace under pressure. When getting to the root of the problem encourage him to explore and examine his feelings in a healthy way. He may find that what he thought was bothering him actually points to something far less complicated or troubling. For example, say your son comes home from a weekend sleepover at his best friend, Nathaniel's house. Instead of telling you about all the cool things they did he instead drops his bags on the floor and flops into a nearby chair, scowling. When you ask him how it went at Nathaniel's he rolls his eyes and says "I don't know...not great. Whatever." At this point it is helpful to change tack and ask your child how he feels and would he like to talk about it. Instead of answering directly he responds with "Ever since Nathaniel got accepted into Duke he has no time for me and he's always talking about college. I told him Duke sucks and he got mad so whatever."

Now, as an adult, you probably understand what is really going on in this conflict. But before you try to help your child untangle his frustration, first commiserate with him about how he feels. He should know that you are really sorry that he feels bad and that his weekend was not a good one. Then you can remind him that he had also considered Duke at one point but had changed his mind in favor of schools in the northeast. Remind him that it was Nathaniel who suggested they hang out over the weekend before midterms consumed all of his time. Perhaps your child is upset at the thought of his best friends going away to college hundreds of miles away. Perhaps he is anxious because although college is still two years away for him and he worries about getting into a good school. Regardless of the actual basis for the conflict, he can not get to it unless he learns how to separate how he feels from what is actually taking place. Help him process the conflict and then leave it up to him to find some healthy ways to approach resolution. If he still needs your help he will let you know.

Your child needs to know that, when others anger or disappoint him, he should deal with the offending behavior, and refrain from attacking the person. As he learns this, his ability to deal with the emotions around a conflict will also improve. Ultimately, regulating his reactions and treating people with respect, even when they are behaving in a way that is hurtful or unfair, will become second nature.

Younger children can be started along this road by continually emphasizing to them that they are entitled to their feelings and emotions and but that their behaviors should be controlled. Send a clear message to your child that how he feels is important to you, but also that you will not condone negative behavior just because he is frustrated or angry. Encourage him to tell you what is bothering him, how he feels and what he would like to see happen. If the outcomes he desires are reasonable, show him ways to achieve them. For example, you may never realize that your five year old is flinging his toys against the wall because it is no longer working and the batteries need to be replaced if you only swoop in to deal with the tantrum itself.

Once you have stopped the behavior let your child know you are ready to hear his line of reasoning. It may take some prompting from you as children cannot always connect the dots between their emotions and their actions. Once the real problem is understood ask him what he thinks would be the appropriate solution. This puts him in the driver's seat and as he grows he will become adept at independent problem-solving and action-based resolutions.

If what he wants is unreasonable - for example, he may tell you that he wants all new toys - tell him so and why. This is also a good opportunity to try to divert his attention to other, more pleasant activities. If he is still unwilling to cooperate simply give him the space and time he needs to manage his disappointment or frustration. Arguing, over-explaining, cajoling or threatening punishment will

102

only intensify the situation and will poke holes in the boundaries you have set between acceptable and unacceptable behavior.

Lastly, don't forget that a little humor goes a long way in diffusing intense situations and making otherwise frustrating circumstances a little easier to deal with. And do not underestimate the power of the once-in-a-blue-moon freebie - the completely unmerited and unexpected pardon we give people we love when they have done something they clearly know deserves our frustration. It can show your child that you realize everyone makes mistakes and that, sometimes, there is no harm in simply calling a truce, shaking hands and calling it a day.

Dealing with Difficult Subjects

At every stage of development your child will be faced with confusing, upsetting or complicated issues. He will need guidance and information as he navigates unfamiliar waters. As he grows, however, it will become increasingly likely that he will look to his peers and other members of his social group for their take on tricky subjects. This is to be expected but the information that comes to your child in way may be of questionable veracity. Thus it is important that, when he does turn to you, you make the interaction a beneficial one.

Unless the topic deals with safety and health issues, it is important to let him raise it with you himself. This gives him equal ownership of the discussion which, in turn, will make him more likely to consider what you tell him carefully. For example, you would delve into the issue of underage drug and alcohol use without waiting for him to bring it up, but a question about how to let a crush know you're interested is one your child would presumably bring to you.

Sex, death, politics, race, war and religion - these are examples of hot button issues your child will need your guidance to navigate. Topics like these can be fraught with controversy and understanding them will give him a firm foundation upon which to form his own beliefs and opinions as he grows. Discussions of these issues are opportunities to expand his view of the world and help him face the adversities that are a part of the human condition. Personal preferences, your family's values and your child's personality will all dictate the tone and content of your conversation.

These exchanges should be conducted with openness and, hopefully, a sense of humor. Direct your child to sources from which he can find out more about a topic. It is extremely important that you frame your conversation with your child in a way that precludes judgement or sanctimony, neither of which will help your child to become compassionate or open-minded. Whatever your views may be on the topic, explain to him why you feel that way. Follow this by telling him that he should not expect all families to feel the same way or hold the same views. Different opinions and those who hold them should be respected, even when we don't agree with them.

If your child springs a surprise question or topic on you and you need a moment to compose your response tell him that you think he has asked an excellent question and you will be happy to discuss it with him after lunch or after he brings down his laundry or after you make a quick cup of tea. This response is far better than appearing flushed, embarrassed or deflective. If you become flustered or rattled this will tell your child that the topic is anxiety-provoking or taboo and may make him less likely to share things with you in the future. Actively listen and make sure you get a clear sense of not only what he thinks but how he feels. Without probing too insistently, calmly try to determine what situation lead to his question. This will give you important details about what is influencing him and to what he is being exposed.

Commend him for his curiosity and thank him for coming to you with the question. Ask him if he has further questions. If he does not ask him to paraphrase the main points you have made. This will let you know whether he has truly understood you or simply wants the conversation to be over. If necessary, tell your child you will locate additional resources or materials for you both to review.

In rare cases when he has confided in you about something that may threaten his immediate safety or well-being, or of that of a friend, take action without delay. Notify any and all individuals who need to be aware of the situation and explain to your child that he has done something commendable by bringing the situation to your attention.

Remaining positive and relaxed in awkward moments will teach your child to do the same, making him less likely to be tense, overly dramatic or embarrassed when sticky situations come up - another important sign of maturity. This layer of growth will help distinguish him among his peers. A child in control of his emotions is one who has been taught the importance of engaging with and processing conflict in a healthy way.

Chapter 14
The Sophisticated Traveler

"The world is a book and those who do not travel read only a page."
Saint Augustine

Throughout this book we have emphasized the importance of new experiences for your child. We've described different ways to introduce these experiences during the course of everyday living. However, there is no better way to give your child an array of experiences than to remove him from his everyday life and take him to new places. Travel will be a crucial component to your child's growth and development.

Travel has long been established as a hallmark of sophistication because it affords us a firsthand opportunity to delve into some of the most fascinating and intriguing experiences the world has to offer. It broadens not only the horizons but the heart and mind as well. It will create amazing memories you and your child can treasure for a lifetime.

The child who is familiar with the world around him has a great advantage in life. He becomes informed in ways that books and classrooms cannot often provide. A child with first hand experiences beyond his immediate environment can contribute to discussions and provide insights that other children cannot.

So can sophisticated travelers come only from families who can afford trips to foreign countries? Absolutely not! It is true that the opportunity to travel internationally gives children a tremendous head start on the road to sophistication, but with your guidance regional and local trips can provide many of the same benefits.

Your child should make trips to historical sites in his own state. Often, state capitals have museums dedicated specifically to the state's history. Universities house topical collections pertaining to the social, political, and cultural history of the region, as well. While a good school may provide field trips to such places if they are relatively close to home, families can go further; perhaps make a weekend of it and sprinkle in some purely fun and frivolous destinations along the way. Stopping for lunch and taking selfies with the 8 foot tall plastic lumberjack outside the diner has a charm all its own!

Local and regional travel is an excellent way to explore culture and customs. For example, a family living in the Napa valley in California could, without much planning, pack a picnic lunch and visit a local vineyard. Your child does not have to be old enough to drink wine to appreciate its contribution to the culture and commerce of the area. A discussion of the wine industry in this context has as much potential to broaden your his horizons as does a trip beyond the country's borders.

A parent who stays abreast of what her child is learning in school can easily integrate travel with the lessons. A trip to Washington, DC would be a great choice for a family vacation the summer before your child studies American history or government and politics. The direct experience with national history and current politics not only makes the lessons more accessible, it provides your child with a deeper, more sophisticated grasp of the nuances of the material.

Make it a point to visit regions that differ culturally and geographically. Children who can flourish in different environments are poised for success. A ski trip to Aspen, Colorado with its snow-covered peaks and alpine lifestyle would contrast wonderfully with a trip to Louisiana to experience the rich cultural complexities of New Orleans. A child who has enjoyed a trip steeped in history and the trappings of a very different culture -- a tour of Montreal, for example -- may benefit from a trip that emphasizes the natural world, like a snorkelling junket in the Caribbean or a stay in the Blue Ridge Mountains.

Comparisons and diversity of experience will enhance his ability to think critically. The differences he observes, along with explanations for them, will facilitate the larger connections he makes in his mind as he matures. Part of the confidence exuded by polished children comes from not being intimidated by new things. Understanding the world through travel helps your child see his place in the world, with all of its variety and beauty.

It is important not to overschedule your vacations as this prevents your child from getting the most from the experience. A day full of tourist stops can rob him of the opportunity for those small, unexpected gems of spontaneity -- a gelato with the charming elderly lady who runs the gift shop in Naples, an impromptu French lesson at a cafe in Tours. Rather than making sure that your child sees every renowned monument or museum in a particular area, encourage him instead to engage with the locals, such as chatting with shopkeepers and merchants. Conversing with the people who actually live, work and raise their families in an area is the very best way to learn about what makes that place unique.

Children need time to absorb their impressions and process them, even when the experiences are thrilling and sought after. A relaxed attitude when traveling will give him a chance to compartmentalize what he is seeing, hearing, tasting, feeling and learning. This will make his excursions a much more pleasant experience.

When trips are well planned, the benefits for you child can start well before the journey begins. Once you have decided on a destination, start the process of educating him about the upcoming trip. Travel guides, brochures and internet articles are a great way to familiarize him with the distinctive characteristics and attractions of the part of the globe he will be exploring. This will build his anticipation and give him an emotional investment in seeing the sites for himself. Again, incorporate aspects of the trip into subject matter he has covered or is currently covering at school.

With a little foresight and planning, trips and vacations can even be built around areas you know your child will be studying. A trip to Greece would be an equally excellent culmination of a semester's worth of studies in mythology or philosophy. After completing a complicated thesis on the development of American theater, imagine how exciting a trip to New York City would be for your teen.

Make him a partner in your research. Based on your discussions determine what his expectations are and think about the things he would enjoy seeing and doing. His introduction to other cultures does not have to be purely academic. Before the big trip visit a museum exhibition featuring artifacts from your destination or have dinner at a restaurant that prepares the region's particular cuisine. What is it about the ingredients or cooking techniques involved that make the food unique to that region?

It is important to talk to him about any problems or issues the people of your destination may be dealing with. Explain to him what particular social, economic, political or natural phenomena gave rise to the conditions that affect the area. Has the country or region experienced drought or flooding? What industry supports the local economy? What is the standard of living for the majority of people living and working there?

This information will give your child a frame of reference for what he sees and experiences and will prevent him from viewing his travels as simply a string of tourist attractions created for his enjoyment. His awareness will give him that particular kind of enlightenment that most children his age have not been exposed to - a positive example of continual learning leading to growth and sophistication.

While on the trip remind him of people he cares about at home who will be interested in what the trip was like. Encourage him to think about whether these people might like a souvenir from your travel destination. He should select items that will be of real interest to the recipient. This requires more thought and effort than simply grabbing a handful of keychains or snow globes in the gift shop - it will challenge him to use his intuition, his memory and his imagination.

It is a great idea to help him chronicle his travel experiences. Journaling, photography, scrapbooking, sketching, blogging and videography are all excellent ways to memorialize an exciting adventure. These activities promote observation, analysis and self-expression, and they put your child in control of framing his own impressions. Make time after the trip to let him share these recollections with you. You may find that you and he have two very different impressions of the same events.

A sophisticated traveler is one who has learned how to minimize the journey's inconveniences and maximize its enjoyment. Thus, you should involve your child in the more practical aspects of travel. Explain the steps your journey will entail and what is to be expected. For example, going through airport security will not seem daunting to a younger child once he understands the steps. For older children make sure they help expedite the process and respect the time of others by being alert and prepared. The people behind him at the security checkpoint will not be happy waiting for him to finish his beverage and send one more quick text before starting the scanning process.

Children who are old enough to read are also old enough to assist with packing. Help your child create his own packing list for your upcoming trip. He should imagine his day from beginning to end and jot down what personal items and clothing will be necessary for him to pack. Remind him to consider such things as the weather and any activities that have been planned. After reviewing the list with him give him feedback on any omissions or additions. It may take some time but, sooner than you might imagine, your child will be packing for trips all by himself.

Children should have their own rolling suitcase, carry-on, overnight bag and shoulder bag or purse. A zippered or hanging toiletry bag with waterproof compartments is also a travel essential.

Because the loss of certain items can spell disaster for a trip, these items should remain with you until your child is older and a more experienced traveler. Such items include medications and essential documents (passports, visas, birth certificates).

Manners are as important during travel as at any other time. Sometimes the excitement of a highly anticipated trip and the novelty of the experience can lead a child to forget himself. It happens. Just consistently remind him that the same behavior you expect from him at home needs to be on display during his journey. Everyone he encounters on his trip, from flight personnel to tour guides, should be treated with courtesy and respect.

Chapter 15
Community and Volunteerism

"Our ambitions must be broad enough to include the aspirations and needs of others, for their sakes and for our own."
Cesar Chavez

As you work to ensure that your child becomes a valued family member, friend, and student you will eventually want him to expand his public persona to become a valued member of the community as a whole. Every truly sophisticated person has some measure of community involvement and, like such people, your child will benefit immensely from making connections to something bigger than himself.

Social Responsibility

You have already made your child aware of his social obligations and he has worked hard to learn the manners and comportment necessary for him to make a good impression, show courtesy and give others respect. Community involvement is a wonderful next step for your child to undertake.

As always, civility is the order of the day for any social interaction, all the more so for interactions that occur in public. Your child should have a working knowledge of basic public conduct and know what is expected of him when he is out and about. Horseplay in public spaces that are not intended for that purpose is antithetical to good manners. Make sure your child is aware that standing on benches, littering, polluting public fountains, and using recreational equipment on sidewalks are all simply not acceptable. Reinforce this lesson when you are out together. Climbing onto public works or community arts projects such as statues is both dangerous and unruly. Shouting, playing loud music and using of profanity in public are absolutely prohibited.

Running on public streets is dangerous to your child and to others and should only happen in emergencies. Teach him to walk on the right hand side of lanes and sidewalks without skipping, jumping, hopping, zig-zagging or making any other erratic or unpredictable movements. He must be aware of those around him. Small children, the elderly, and mobility-impaired persons may not always follow the expected pattern when moving down the sidewalk. Teach your child to take responsibility for avoiding mishaps.

It used to be common to teach children to assist individuals who seemed in need of it. Times and attitudes have changed, however. Your child's safety is your first priority and so you may choose to restrict him from helping people in public. The possibility for him to sustain an injury is always present and the emotional and legal ramifications of unintentionally hurting someone he was trying to help could be serious and ongoing. Perhaps you will decide that he should only offer assistance if you are nearby. You must weigh the options yourself to come up with a family practice that works for you and your child.

Inclusivity and Diversity

There will be times when your younger child may seem confused or overly curious when he encounters an individual he finds to be unusual for any number of reasons. For example, say you are on the train and your child sees a woman with no legs seated in a wheelchair. He asks you what happened to the woman or why doesn't she have any legs. Despite your initial reaction of embarrassment or discomfort you should simply tell your child that you do not know and try to refocus his attention on whatever task he was engaged in before. If this proves to be ineffective and he continues to ask questions simply say "I don't know, but it's okay if we do not know everything about everyone we meet, don't you agree?"

Once you are home have a conversation with him about boundaries and being respectful of others. Your child is not rude; he is simply uninformed and inexperienced. Explain to him that some

113

people dress, move, speak, hear, see and behave in many different ways. Some of these ways may stand out because they seem different, but different does not equal wrong. One thing that can be considered wrong, however, is discussing people we see in public. He should know that doing so may make people feel awkward or uncomfortable so we simply must not do it.

Of the course of his young life, your child will inevitably encounter many people who are different from him in one way or another - different races, ethnic backgrounds, nationalities, gender identities, and lifestyle preferences. Teach your child to value this diversity and see it as part of what makes life, and people, interesting. The sophisticated child is confident and strong enough to be secure and accepting of others.

Again, this is another area in which your example will have a great influence. If your child is regularly exposed to people of different backgrounds and cultures, he not only will be accepting of diversity, he will see it as normative. This attitude will keep him open in the future to opportunities to meet and become friends with a wide variety of interesting people -- another mark of the sophisticate!

It is best to be honest with him about prejudice. Explain that others may have different and strong opinions about accepting others. Sometimes it will take courage and integrity to befriend people who seem different from us.

Say your child tells you that his classmates taunted a new student because she is foreign-born and of a different ethnicity. You can see that he is upset about what happened. Tell him that you wish his friends felt differently about the opportunity to make a new friend. Ask him if he thinks any of those friends would refuse to open a birthday gift because they did not like the paper it was wrapped in. He will agree that that is silly and you will be one step closer in helping him understand the error of his friends' thinking. It would not be appropriate to forbid him from associating with his friends because of their views. It is far more important to explain to your child why you feel the way you do and what lessons you want him to absorb.

Banning him from the company of his friends at school sends the message that people who feel and think differently than he and his family should be punished or ostracized. It may also make him feel less willing to come to you in the future with problems. While it can be upsetting to know that children with such different views are friends with your child, you should realize that the example you have set means that he likely is truly learning right from wrong and will be just fine when he is out on his own. Also, he will have more opportunities to be a positive influence on his friends if he is still in contact with them. This teaches him that we do not have to change people in order to accept them but we do not have to be exactly like them, either.

Encourage him to exercise his good judgement and compassion and find ways to make the new student feel welcome. Our humanity is more than enough reason to celebrate our similarities and find common ground.

Community Involvement

Getting your child involved in the community has many benefits. It will help him to become knowledgeable about local culture and customs, and it will keep him up on current events in the area as well. It also allows him to personal bonds with the people in his environment. There are many ways to get your child involved. Fairs, festivals and community performances are some of the many events in which he can participate.

Make it a practice to introduce him to others when out and about. Soon he will know and be comfortable speaking with his doctor and dentist, the mail carrier, his barber, the crossing guard at school, the waiters at his favorite local restaurant, and so on. These social practices will sharpens his memory and make social interactions more natural to him. In addition, he will leave a good impression with the people he meets.

When appropriate, participate with your child in celebrations and holidays of other cultures. You should always be certain that this will not conflict with any religious prohibitions. For example, only Muslims can participate in certain sacred observances during Ramadan. Likewise, educate your child about cultural appropriation and the respect with which we must approach the cultures of other peoples. For example, a halo war bonnet is a powerful symbol of history, religious and ethnic pride for many Native Peoples and as such should not be worn by anyone other than recognized leaders from those communities. Sharing this information with your child will help him understand that the clothes, practices and rituals of other groups are not to be used as costumes or props by non-members.

Nonetheless, most cultures have customs, rituals and observances that they are proud and eager to share with the world and a bit of research will help you and your child discover them. Celebrating the achievements and contributions of different cultures teaches your child to value and respect these groups and the role they have played in history of his own country.

Have conversations with your child about issues affecting the community. Who is the current mayor? Why are taxpayers upset about the cost of the proposed water treatment plant? How did last summer's drought hurt the local tourism industry? These may not be the most thrilling topics for either you or your child, but he will absorb more of this information than you think. Over time he will become much more knowledgeable about his community than most children of his age.

Community Based Activities

Attend opposing political rallies or campaign functions with your child. Ask him what he thinks about the candidate and how did he think the audience responded? After the election ask your child whether or not he is surprised by the results based on what he previously observed at the rallies.

Bundle up, grab a thermos of cocoa and head downtown for the annual holiday parade sponsored by your city. Discuss the themes and symbols you see and use this as an opportunity to discuss the role religion plays, if at all, as a part of the culture of a community.

Plan a walking tour of your city, or a significant portion of it, with your child. Depending on the size of your community this could take a few weekends or a few months. If it happens to be an area you were familiar with before the birth of your child share your memories with him and discuss which things have or have not changed.

Volunteerism

Volunteering is a way for your child to show empathy and compassion for others while doing his part to make a difference. Teach him that time spent giving back to his community produces lasting and positive results that help everyone, not just the volunteers or those in need of assistance.

For smaller children finding volunteer projects with clear goals and evident results is the best way to communicate the effectiveness of their efforts. Clearing a local park of trash and debris is an age-appropriate task that your younger child can easily understand. For older children extend this approach to more challenging concepts such as nutritional outreach, adult literacy services and animal shelter support. For teens, issues-based projects such as those associated with substance abuse problems, cancer research or domestic violence initiatives can be added to the possibilities for involvement.

Volunteer opportunities can be matched to your child's skill-sets as well. If your son is a pianist he can look into the possibility of performing on Sunday afternoons at a retirement home. A child who enjoys sports could volunteer at a summer camp for under-resourced neighborhoods. A budding artist could assist with an arts and crafts fair for developmentally challenged youth. If the perfect program does not exist, help your child look into the feasibility of creating one.

Volunteering is an extension of community involvement. Understanding this prevents us from feeling like we are superior to those we seek to help. As a conscientious parent, never use the misfortunes of others as a cautionary tale for your child. This displays a lack of empathy and understanding and makes assumptions about the disadvantaged that your child will pick up on and emulate.

If he spends every other weekend volunteering in the local shelter's meal program he should be doing so because he feels he wants to help. Telling him that he could end up in the same situation as the homeless unless he improves his grades will contrast sharply with what you want him to learn by volunteering. He will begin to lose compassion and instead see the setbacks suffered by others as the preventable and well-deserved results of their own mistakes and poor choices. In actuality, your child has no knowledge about the pasts of the people he is helping. And their pasts have nothing to do with the reasons for volunteering.

With a little planning, getting your child involved in his community will make him wiser, more compassionate and more informed. These qualities are important to his maturity and growth and will add to his foundation for future success and yes, sophistication!

Conclusion

"Instruction does much, but encouragement, everything."
Johann Wolfgang von Goethe

As a parent you understand the importance of raising your child to be an engaging, respectful and sophisticated individual. You appreciate the difference it will make in her development as she embraces new opportunities and navigates new challenges with confidence. You recognize the positive effect this will have on her character, her interpersonal relationships and the lenses through which others view her and her contributions.

The time, energy and thoughtfulness you will put into this endeavor will be well worth it as you watch your child blossom into the person you have always known she could be.

We thank you for the opportunity to have this conversation and we wish you and your child happiness, fulfillment and success on this journey.

Parents are a particular lot and they tend to trust the advice and suggestions of other parents. We love this fact - word of mouth recommendations have made our jobs as parents much easier over the years as well. So if you enjoyed the book and think others would enjoy it also. please leave your thoughts and impressions at http://www.amazon.com/Beyond-Good-Manners-Raise-Sophisticated-ebook/dp/B01CS6OZG8/ref=asap_bc?ie=UTF8

Thank you for reading "Beyond Good Manners: How to Raise a Sophisticated Child" by Tara Woods Turner and J. Blake Turner, PhD.

www.ingramcontent.com/pod-product-compliance
Lightning Source LLC
Chambersburg PA
CBHW031517040426
42445CB00009B/269